Renew online at
www.librarieswest.org.uk
or by phoning any Bristol library

Bristol Libraries

PLEASE RETURN BOOK BY LAST DATE STAMPED

D1350478

Credits

Footprint credits
Editorial: Jo Williams
Proofreader: Sophie Jones
Maps: Kevin Feeney
Cover: Pepi Bluck

Publisher: Patrick Dawson
Managing Editor: Felicity Laughton
Advertising: Elizabeth Taylor
Sales and marketing: Kirsty Holmes

Photography credits
Front cover: Dariusz Gora/Shutterstock.com
Back cover: Laurence Gough/Shutterstock.com

Printed in Great Britain by CPI Antony Rowe, Chippenham, Wiltshire

FSC
www.fsc.org

MIX
Paper from
responsible sources
FSC® C013604

Publishing information
Footprint *Focus Norfolk, Suffolk & Cambridge*
1st edition
© Footprint Handbooks Ltd
April 2013

ISBN: 978 1 909268 18 0
CIP DATA: A catalogue record for this book is available from the British Library

® Footprint Handbooks and the Footprint mark are a registered trademark of Footprint Handbooks Ltd

Published by Footprint
6 Riverside Court
Lower Bristol Road
Bath BA2 3DZ, UK
T +44 (0)1225 469141
F +44 (0)1225 469461
footprinttravelguides.com

Distributed in the USA by Globe Pequot Press, Guilford, Connecticut

The content of Footprint *Focus Norfolk, Suffolk & Cambridge* has been updated from Footprint's *England Handbook* which was researched and written by Charlie Godfrey-Faussett.

Contents

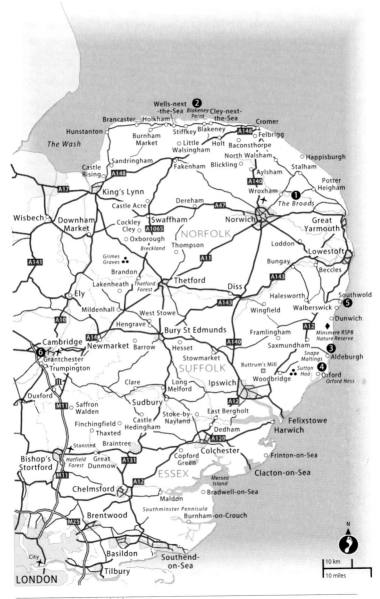

East Anglia is a peculiar corner of England, the closest it comes to Holland: both offbeat and individualist and with almost as settled and civilized an air. Norfolk and Suffolk are its essential counties, although the region can also be said to embrace Essex in the south and Cambridgeshire in the west. Geologically, it's the youngest part of the country and it's also relatively isolated from the rest of the country. It's the endless flat horizons of Norfolk's north coast, Suffolk's eerie seashore and the level watery marshland of the Broads that draw the most discerning visitors.

Cambridge is a hotbed of cutting-edge technological and intellectual activity; Norwich is the home of the flourishing University of East Anglia (UEA) and the world-class Sainsbury Centre of Visual Arts; Suffolk has received a shot in the arm from emigrant Londoners; the towns on its unearthly coastline – Southwold, Dunwich, Aldeburgh, Orford – are all awash with metropolitan gossip; and Essex, well, it's one of the most mixed-up, in-yer-face counties and it's within spitting distance of London: think The Prodigy, Squarepusher and loud, pointy-chested girls as well as the watercolour prettiness of Constable Country. This is the county that embraces both militarized Colchester and the olde-worlde charm of Saffron Walden. The latter sits at the heart of an area endearingly named Uttlesford, including sleepy market towns like Thaxted and Great Dunmow. On the coast to the south, Southend soaks up weekending Eastenders, while, to the east, Clacton and Frinton compete shoulder to shoulder.

Planning your trip

Best time to visit England

The weather in England is generally better between May and September, although it can be gloriously hot in April and cold and damp in August. The west of the country is milder and wetter than the east, whilst northern regions and mountainous areas such as the Peninnes are usually the coldest areas.

Transport in England

Compared to the rest of Western Europe, public transport in England can be expensive. Rail, in particular, is pricey compared to many other European countries. Coach travel is cheaper but much slower, and is further hampered by serious traffic problems around London, Manchester and Birmingham. Some areas, such as the Cotswolds, Peak or Lake District, are poorly served by public transport of any kind, and if you plan to spend much time in rural areas, it may be worth hiring a car, especially if you are travelling as a couple or group. A useful website for all national public transport information is **Traveline** ① *T0871-200 2233, www.traveline.info.*

Air

England is a small country, and air travel isn't strictly necessary to get around. However, with traffic a problem around the cities, some of the cheap fares offered by budget airlines may be very attractive. There are good connections between **London** and all the regional airports, although travel from region to region without coming through London is more difficult and expensive. Bear in mind the time and money it will take you to get to the airport (including check in times) when deciding whether flying is really going to be a better deal.

Airport information National Express operates a frequent service between London's main airports. **London Heathrow Airport** ① *16 miles west of London between junctions 3 and 4 on the M4, T0844-335 1801, www.heathrowairport.com,* is the world's busiest international airport and it has five terminals, so when leaving London, it's important to check which terminal to go to before setting out for the airport. To get into central London, the cheapest option is the London Underground Piccadilly Line (50 minutes). The fastest option is **Heathrow Express** ① *T0845-6001515, www.heathrowexpress.com,* taking 15-20 minutes. There is a train service **Heathrow Connect** ① *Heathrow T0845-748 4950, www.heathrow connect.com,* which takes 25 minutes. Coaches to destinations all over the country are run by **National Express** ① *T0871-781 8181, www.national express.com.* There are also buses to Oxford (www.oxfordbus.co.uk), to Reading for trains to Bristol and southwest England (www.railair.com), to Watford for trains to the north of England (www.greenline.co.uk) and to West London (www.tfl.gov.uk). A taxi to central London takes 1 hour and costs £45-£70.

    London Gatwick Airport ① *28 miles south of London, off junction 9 on the M23, T0844-892 03222, www.gatwickairport.com,* has two terminals, North and South, with all the usual

Don't miss...

facilities. To central London, there is the **Gatwick Express** ① *T0845-850 1530, www.gatwickexpress.com, from £17.75 single online*, which takes 30 minutes. **Thameslink** rail services run from King's Cross, Farringdon, Blackfriars and London Bridge stations. Contact **National Rail Enquiries** (T0845-748 4950, www.nationalrail.co.uk) for further information. **EasyBus** (www.easybus.co.uk) is the cheapest option, with prices at £9.99 single, taking just over an hour. A taxi takes a similar time and costs from around £60.

London City Airport ① *Royal Dock, 6 miles (15 mins' drive) east of the City of London, T020-7646 0000, www.londoncityairport.com*. Take the **Docklands Light Railway** (DLR) to Canning Town (7 minutes) for the **Jubilee line** or a connecting shuttle bus service. A taxi into central London will cost around £35.

London Luton Airport ① *30 miles north of central London, 2 miles off the M1 at junction 10, southeast of Luton, Beds, T01582-405100, www.london-luton.co.uk*. Regular **First Capital Connect** trains run to central London; a free shuttle bus service operates between the airport terminal and the station. **Green Line** (www.greenline.co.uk) coaches run to central London, as does **easyBus** (www.easybus.co.uk). **National Express** (www.nationalexpress.com) operate coaches to many destinations. A taxi takes 50 minutes, costing from £70.

Stansted Airport ① *35 miles northeast of London (near Cambridge) by junction 8 of the M11, T0844-335 1803, www.stanstedairport.com*. **Stansted Express** (T0845-600 7245, www.stanstedexpress.com) runs trains to London's Liverpool Street Station (45 minutes, £22.50 single). **EasyBus** (www.easybus.co.uk, from £2), **Terravision** (www.terravision.eu, £9) and **National Express** (www.nationalexpress.com, from £8.50) run to central London (55 minutes to East London, 1 hour 30 minutes to Victoria). A taxi to central London takes around an hour to 1 hour 30 minutes, depending on traffic, and costs around £99.

Manchester International Airport ① *at junction 5 of the M56, T0871-271 0711, www.manchester airport.co.uk*. The airport is well-served by public transport, with trains to and from Manchester Piccadilly as well as direct and connecting services from all over the north of England. **National Express** (www.nationalexpress.com) runs routes covering the whole of the UK. A taxi into the city centre should cost around £20.

Birmingham International Airport (BHX) ① *8 miles east of the city centre at junction 6 on the M42, T0871-222 0072, www.birminghamairport.co.uk*. A taxi into the centre should cost from £25. Several trains per hour run the free 10-minute Air-Rail Link to Birmingham International Station, and other connections across England and Wales can be made by rail or coach, with **National Express** (www.nationalexpress.com).

Rail

National Rail Enquiries ① T08457-484950, www.nationalrail.co.uk, are quick and courteous with information on rail services and fares but not always accurate, so double check. They can't book tickets but will provide you with the relevant telephone number. The website, www.thetrainline.co.uk, also shows prices clearly.

Railcards There are a variety of railcards which give discounts on fares for certain groups. Cards are valid for one year and most are available from main stations. You need two passport photos and proof of age or status. A Young Person's Railcard is for those aged 16-25 or full-time students aged 26+ in the UK. Costs £28 for one year and gives 33% discount on most train tickets and some other services (www.16-25railcard.co.uk). A Senior Citizen's Railcard is for those aged over 60, is the same price and offers the same discounts as a Young Person's Railcard (www.senior-railcard.co.uk). A Disabled Person's Railcard costs £20 and gives 33% discount to a disabled person and one other. Pick up an application form from stations and send it to Disabled Person's Railcard Office, PO Box 11631, Laurencekirk AB30 9AA. It may take up to 10 working days to be delivered, so apply in advance (www.disabledpersons-railcard.co.uk). A Family & Friends Railcard costs £28 and gives 33% discount on most tickets for up to four adults travelling together, and 60% discount for up to four children. It's available to buy online as well as in most stations.

Road

Bus and coach Travelling by bus takes longer than the train but is much cheaper. Road links between cities and major towns in England are excellent, but far less frequent in more remote rural areas, and a number of companies offer express coach services day and night. The main operator is **National Express** ① T08717-818178, www.national express.com, which has a nationwide network with over 1000 destinations. Tickets can be bought at bus stations, from a huge number of agents throughout the country or online. Sample return fares if booked in advance: London to Manchester (4 hours 35 minutes) £28, London to Cambridge (2 hours 30 mins) £12. **Megabus** ① T0900-1600 900 (61p a min from BT landlines, calls from other networks may be higher), http://megabus.com, is a cheaper alternative with a more limited service.

Full-time students, those aged under 25 or over 60 or those registered disabled, can buy a coach card for £10 which is valid for 1 year and gets you a 30% discount on all fares. Children normally travel for half price, but with a Family Card costing £16, two children travel free with two adults. Available to overseas passport holders, the Brit Xplorer Pass offers unlimited travel on all National Express buses. Passes cost from £79 for seven days, £139 for 14 days and £219 for its month-long Rolling Stone pass. They can be bought from major airports and bus terminals.

Car Travelling with your own private transport is the ideal way to explore the country, particularly in areas badly served by public transport. This allows you to cover a lot of ground in a short space of time and to reach remote places. The main disadvantages are rising fuel costs, parking and traffic congestion. The latter is particularly heavy on the M25 which encircles London, the M6 around Birmingham and the M62 around Manchester. The M4 and M5 motorways to the West Country can also become choked at weekends and bank holidays and the roads in Cornwall often resemble a glorified car park during the summer.

Motoring organizations can help with route planning, traffic advice, insurance and breakdown cover. The two main ones are: the **Automobile Association (AA)** ① *T0800-085 2721, emergency number T0800-887766, www.theaa.com*, which offers a year's breakdown cover starting at £38, and the **Royal Automobile Club (RAC)** ① *T0844-273 4341, emergency number T08000-828282, www.rac.co.uk*, which has a year's breakdown cover starting at £31.99. Both have cover for emergency assistance. You can still call the emergency numbers if you're not a member, but you'll have to a pay a large fee.

Vehicle hire

Car hire is expensive and the minimum you can expect to pay is around £100 per week for a small car. Always check and compare conditions, such as mileage limitations, excess payable in the case of an accident, etc. Small, local hire companies often offer better deals than the larger multinationals. Most companies prefer payment with a credit card – some insist on it – otherwise you'll have to leave a large deposit (£100 or more). You need to have had a full driver's licence for at least a year and to be aged between 21 (25 for some companies) and 70.

Bicycle

Cycling is a pleasant if slightly hazardous way to see the country. Although conditions for cyclists are improving, with a growing network of cycle lanes in cities, most other roads do not have designated cycle paths, and cyclists are not allowed on motorways. You can load your bike onto trains, though some restrictions apply during rush hour. See www.ctc.org.uk for information on routes, restrictions and facilities.

Where to stay in England

Accommodation can mean anything from being pampered to within an inch of your life in a country house spa hotel to glamping in a yurt. If you have the money, then the sky is very much the limit in terms of sheer splendour and excess. We have listed top class establishments in this book, with a bias towards those that offer that little bit extra in terms of character.

We have tried to give as broad a selection as possible to cater for all tastes and budgets but if you can't find what you're after, or if someone else has beaten you to the draw, then the tourist information centres (TICs) will help find accommodation for you. Some offices charge a small fee (usually £1) for booking a room, while others ask you to pay a deposit of 10% which is deducted from your first night's bill. Details of town and city TICs are given throughout the guide.

Accommodation will be your greatest expense, particularly if you are travelling on your own. Single rooms are in short supply and many places are reluctant to let a double room to one person, even when they're not busy. Single rooms are usually more than the cost per person for a double room and sometimes cost the same as two people sharing a double room.

Hotels, guesthouses and B&Bs

Area tourist boards publish accommodation lists that include campsites, hostels, self-catering accommodation, hotels, guesthouses and bed and breakfasts (B&Bs). Places participating in the VisitEngland system will have a plaque displayed outside which shows their grading,

Price codes

Where to stay

££££	over £160	**£££**	£90-160
££	£50-90	**£**	under £50

Prices include taxes and service charge, but not meals. They are based on a double room for one night in high season.

Restaurants

£££	over £30	**££**	£15-30	**£**	under £15

Prices refer to the cost of a two-course meal for one person, without a drink.

determined by a number of stars ranging from one to five. These reflect the level of facilities, as well as the quality of hospitality and service. However, do not assume that a B&B, guesthouse or hotel is no good because it is not listed by the tourist board. They simply don't want to pay to be included in the system, and some of them may offer better value.

Hotels At the top end of the scale there are some fabulously luxurious hotels, some in beautiful locations. Some are converted mansions or castles, and offer a chance to enjoy a taste of aristocratic grandeur and style. At the lower end of the scale, there is often little to choose between cheaper hotels and guesthouses or B&Bs. The latter often offer higher standards of comfort and a more personal service, but many smaller hotels are really just guesthouses, and are often family run and every bit as friendly. Rooms in most mid-range to expensive hotels almost always have bathrooms en suite. Many upmarket hotels offer excellent room-only deals in the low season. An efficient last-minute hotel booking service is www.laterooms.com, which specializes in weekend breaks. Also note that many hotels offer cheaper rates for online booking through agencies such as www.lastminute.com.

Guesthouses Guesthouses are often large, converted family homes with up to five or six rooms. They tend to be slightly more expensive than B&Bs, charging between £30 and £50 per person per night, and though they are often less personal, usually provide better facilities, such as en suite bathroom, TV in each room, free Wi-Fi and private parking. Many guesthouses offer evening meals, though this may have to be requested in advance.

Bed and breakfasts (B&Bs) B&Bs usually provide the cheapest private accommodation. At the bottom end of the scale you can get a bedroom in a private house, a shared bathroom and a huge cooked breakfast from around £25 per person per night. Small B&Bs may only have one or two rooms to let, so it's important to book in advance during the summer season. More upmarket B&Bs, some in handsome period houses, have en suite bathrooms, free Wi-Fi and TVs in each room and usually charge from £35 per person per night.

Hostels

For those travelling on a tight budget, there is a network of hostels offering cheap accommodation in major cities, national parks and other areas of beauty, run by the **Youth Hostel Association (YHA)** ① *T01629-592600, or customer services T0800-0191 700,*

+44-1629 592700 from outside the UK, www.yha.org.uk. Membership costs from £14.35 a year and a bed in a dormitory costs from £15 to £25 a night. They offer bunk-bed accommodation in single-sex dormitories or smaller rooms, as well as family rooms, kitchen and laundry facilities. Though some rural hostels are still strict on discipline and impose a 2300 curfew, those in larger towns and cities tend to be more relaxed and doors are closed as late as 0200. Some larger hostels provide breakfasts for around £2.50 and three-course evening meals for £4-5. You should always phone ahead, as many hostels are closed during the day and phone numbers are listed in this guide. Advance booking is recommended at all times, particularly from May to September and on public holidays. Many hostels are closed during the winter. Youth hostel members are entitled to various discounts, including tourist attractions and travel. The YHA also offer budget self-catering bunkhouses with mostly dorm accommodation and some family rooms, which are in more rural locations. Camping barns, camping pods and camping are other options offered by the YHA; see the website for details.

Details of most independent hostels can be found in the *Independent Hostel Guide* (T01629-580427, www.independenthostelguide.co.uk). Independent hostels tend to be more laid-back, with fewer rules and no curfew, and no membership is required. They all have dorms, hot showers and self-catering kitchens, and some have family and double rooms. Some include continental breakfast, or offer cheap breakfasts.

Self-catering accommodation
There are lots of different types of accommodation to choose from, to suit all budgets, ranging from luxury lodges, castles and lighthouses to basic cottages. Expect to pay at least £200-400 per week for a two-bedroom cottage in the winter, rising to £400-1000 in the high season, or more if it's a particularly nice place. A good source of information on self-catering accommodation is the VisitEngland website, www.visitengland.com, and its *VisitEngland Self-catering 2013* guide, which lists many properties and is available to buy from any tourist office and many bookshops, but there are also dozens of excellent websites to browse. Amongst the best websites are: www.cottages4you.co.uk, www.ruralretreats.co.uk and www.ownersdirect.co.uk. If you want to tickle a trout or feed a pet lamb, **Farm Stay UK** (www.farmstay.co.uk) offer over a thousand good value rural places to stay around England, all clearly listed on a clickable map.

More interesting places to stay are offered by the **Landmark Trust** ① *T01628-825925, www.landmarktrust.org.uk*, who rent out renovated historic landmark buildings, from atmospheric castles to cottages, and the **National Trust** ① *T0844-800 2070, www.nationaltrustcottages.co.uk*, who provide a wide variety of different accommodation on their estates. A reputable agent for self-catering cottages is **English Country Cottages** ① *T0845-268 0785, www.english-country-cottages.co.uk*.

Campsites
Campsites vary greatly in quality and level of facilities. Some sites are only open from April to October. See the following sites: www.pitchup.com; www.coolcamping.com, good for finding characterful sites that allow campfires; www.ukcampsite.co.uk, which is the most comprehensive service with thousands of sites, many with pictures and reviews from punters; and www.campingandcaravanningclub.co.uk. The Forestry Commission have campsites on their wooded estates, see www.campingintheforest.com.

Food and drink in England

Food

Only 30 years ago few would have thought to come to England for haute cuisine. Since the 1980s, though, the English have been determinedly shrugging off their reputation for over-boiled cabbage and watery beef. Now cookery shows like Masterchef are the most popular on TV after the soaps, and thanks in part to the wave of celebrity chefs they have created, you can expect a generally high standard of competence in restaurant kitchens. Towns like Ludlow, Padstow and Whitstable have carved reputations for themselves almost solely on the strength of their cuisine.

Pub food has also been transformed in recent years, and now many of them offer ambitious lunchtime and supper menus in so-called gastro pubs. Most parts of the country still boast regional specialities, including succulent Colchester oysters and Cromer crabs. Other specialities are spankingly fresh seafood, especially oysters, winkles, and mussels Norfolk, as well as fish from the sea – often bass, mullet and sole – and from the farm – trout and salmon, mainly.

The biggest problem with eating out is the ludicrously limited serving hours in some pubs and hotels, particularly in remoter locations. These places only serve food during restricted hours, generally about 1200-1430 for lunch and 1830-2130 for supper, seemingly ignorant of the eating habits of foreign visitors, or those who would prefer a bit more flexibility during their holiday. In small places especially, it can be difficult finding food outside these enforced times. Places that serve food all day till 2100 or later are restaurants, fast-food outlets and the many chic bistros and café-bars, which can be found not only in the main cities but increasingly in smaller towns. The latter often offer very good value and above-average quality fare.

Drink

Drinking is a national hobby and sometimes a dangerous one at that. **Real ale** – flat, brown beer known as bitter, made with hops – is the national drink, but now struggles to maintain its market share in the face of fierce competition from continental lagers and alcopops. Many small independent breweries are still up and running though, as well as microbreweries attached to individual pubs, which produce far superior ales. **Cider** (fermented apple juice) is also experiencing a resurgence of interest and is a speciality of Somerset. English **wine** is also proving surprisingly resilient: generally it compares favourably with German varieties and many vineyards now offer continental-style sampling sessions.

In many pubs the basic ales are chilled under gas pressure like lagers, but the best ales, such as those from the independents, are 'real ales', still fermenting in the cask and served cool but not chilled (around 12°C) under natural pressure from a handpump, electric pump or air pressure fount.

The **pub** is still the traditional place to enjoy a drink: the best are usually freehouses (not tied to a brewery) and feature real log or coal fires in winter, flower-filled gardens for the summer (even in cities occasionally) and most importantly, thriving local custom. Many also offer characterful accommodation and restaurants serving high-quality fare. Pubs are prey to the same market forces as any other business, though, and many a delightful local has recently succumbed to exorbitant property prices or to the bland makeover favoured by the large chains. In 2012, pubs were closing at the rate of 12 a week due to the recession.

Essentials A-Z

Accident and emergency

For police, fire brigade, ambulance and, in certain areas, mountain rescue or coastguard, T999 or T112.

Disabled travellers

Wheelchair users, and blind or partially sighted people are automatically given 34-50% discount on train fares, and those with other disabilities are eligible for the Disabled Person's Railcard, which costs £20 per year and gives a third off most tickets. If you will need assistance at a railway station, call the train company that manages the station you're starting your journey from 24 hours in advance. **Disabled UK** residents can apply to their local councils for a concessionary bus pass. National Express have a helpline for disabled passengers, T08717-818179, to plan journeys and arrange assistance. They also sell a discount coach card for £10 for people with disabilities.

The **English Tourist Board** website, www.visitengland.com, has information on the National Accessible Scheme (NAS) logos to help disabled travellers find the right accommodation for their needs, as well as details of walks that are possible with wheelchairs and the Shopmobility scheme. Many local tourist offices offer accessibility details for their area.

Useful organizations include:
Radar, T020-7250 3222, www.radar.org.uk. A good source of advice and information. It produces an annual National Key Scheme Guide and key for gaining access to over 9000 toilet facilities across the UK.
Tourism for all, T0845-124 9971, www.holidaycare.org.uk, www.tourismfor all.org.uk. An excellent source of information about travel and for identifying accessible accommodation in the UK.

Electricity

The current in Britain is 240V AC. Plugs have 3 square pins and adapters are widely available.

Health

For minor accidents go to the nearest casualty department or an Accident and Emergency (A&E) Unit at a hospital. For other enquiries phone NHS Direct 24 hours (T0845-4647) or visit an NHS walk-in centre. See also individual town and city directories throughout the book for details of local medical services.

Money→ *For up-to-date exhange rates, see* www.xe.com.
The British currency is the pound sterling (£), divided into 100 pence (p). Coins come in denominations of 1p, 2p, 5p, 10p, 20p, 50p, £1 and £2. Banknotes come in denominations of £5, £10, £20 and £50. The last of these is not widely used and may be difficult to change.

Banks and bureaux de change

Banks tend to offer similar exchange rates and are usually the best places to change money and cheques. Outside banking hours you'll have to use a bureau de change, which can be easily found at the airports and train stations and in larger cities. **Thomas Cook** and other major travel agents also operate bureaux de change with reasonable rates. Avoid changing money or cheques in hotels, as the rates are usually poor. Main post offices and branches of **Marks and Spencer** will change cash without charging commission.

Credit cards and ATMs

Most hotels, shops and restaurants accept the major credit cards though some places may charge for using them. Some smaller establishments such as B&Bs may only accept cash.

Currency cards

If you don't want to carry lots of cash, prepaid currency cards allow you to preload money from your bank account, fixed at the day's exchange rate. They look like a credit or debit card and are issued by specialist money changing companies, such as **Travelex** and **Caxton FX**. You can top up and check your balance by phone, online and sometimes by text.

Money transfers

If you need money urgently, the quickest way to have it sent to you is to have it wired to the nearest bank via **Western Union**, T0800-833833, www.westernunion.co.uk, or **MoneyGram**, www.moneygram.com. The Post Office can also arrange a MoneyGram transfer. Charges are on a sliding scale; so it will cost proportionately less to wire out more money. Money can also be wired by **Thomas Cook**, www.thomasexchangeglobal.co.uk, or transferred via a bank draft, but this can take up to a week.

Taxes

Most goods are subject to a Value Added Tax (VAT) of 20%, with the major exception of food and books. VAT is usually already included in the advertised price of goods. Visitors from non-EU countries can save money through shopping at places that offer Tax Free Shopping (also known as the Retail Export Scheme), which allows a refund of VAT on goods that will be taken out of the country. Note that not all shops participate in the scheme and that VAT cannot be reclaimed on hotel bills or other services.

Cost of travelling

England can be an expensive place to visit, and London and the south in particular can eat heavily into your budget. There is budget accommodation available, however, and backpackers will be able to keep their costs down. Fuel is a major expense and won't just cost an arm and a leg but also the limbs of all remaining family members, and public transport – particularly rail travel if not booked in advance – can also be pricey, especially for families. Accommodation and restaurant prices also tend to be higher in more popular destinations and during the busy summer months.

The minimum daily budget required, if you're staying in hostels or camping, cycling or hitching (not recommended), and cooking your own meals, will be around £30 per person per day. If you start using public transport and eating out occasionally that will rise to around £35-40. Those staying in slightly more upmarket B&Bs or guesthouses, eating out every evening at pubs or modest restaurants and visiting tourist attractions can expect to pay around £60 per day. If you also want to hire a car and eat well, then costs will rise considerably to at least £75-80 per person per day. Single travellers will have to pay more than half the cost of a double room, and should budget on spending around 60-70% of what a couple would spend.

Opening hours

Businesses are usually open Mon-Sat 0900-1700. In towns and cities, as well as villages in holiday areas, many shops open on a Sun but they will open later and close earlier. For banks, see above. For TIC opening hours, see the tourist information sections in the relevant cities, towns and villages in the text.

Post

Most post offices are open Mon-Fri 0900 to 1730 and Sat 0900-1230 or 1300. Smaller sub-post offices are closed for an hour at lunch (1300-1400) and many of them operate out of a shop. Stamps can be bought at post offices, but also from many shops. A 1st-class letter weighing up to 100 g to anywhere in the UK costs 60p (a large letter over 240 mm by 165 mm is 90p) and should arrive the following day, while 2nd-class letters weighing up to 100 g cost 50p (69p) and take between 2-4 days. For more information about Royal Mail postal services, call T08457-740740, or visit www.royalmail.com.

Safety
Generally speaking, England is a safe place to visit. English cities have their fair share of crime, but much of it is drug-related and confined to the more deprived peripheral areas. Trust your instincts, and if in doubt, take a taxi.

Telephone → Country code +44.
Useful numbers: operator T100; international operator T155; directory enquiries T192; overseas directory enquiries T153.

Most public payphones are operated by British Telecom (**BT**) and can be found in towns and cities, though less so in rural areas. Numbers of public phone booths have declined in recent years due to the advent of the mobile phone, so don't rely on being able to find a payphone wherever you go. Calls from BT payphones cost a minimum of 60p, for which you get 30 mins for a local or national call. Calls to non-geographic numbers (eg 0845), mobile phones and others may cost more. Payphones take either coins (10p, 20p, 50p and £1), 50c, 1 or 2 euro coins, credit cards or BT Chargecards, which are available at newsagents and post offices displaying the BT logo. These cards come in denominations of £2, £3, £5 and £10. Some payphones also have facilities for internet, text messaging and emailing.

For most countries (including Europe, USA and Canada) calls are cheapest Mon-Fri between 1800 and 0800 and all day Sat-Sun. For Australia and New Zealand it's cheapest to call from 1430-1930 and from 2400-0700 every day. However, the cheapest ways to call abroad from England is not via a standard UK landline provider. Calls are free using **Skype** on the internet, or you can route calls from your phone through the internet with **JaJah** (www.jajah.com) or from a mobile using **Rebtel**. Many phone companies offer discounted call rates by calling their access number prior to dialling the number you want, including www.dialabroad.co.uk and www.simply-call.com.

Area codes are not needed if calling from within the same area. Any number prefixed by 0800 or 0500 is free to the caller; 08457 numbers are charged at local rates and 08705 numbers at the national rate.

Time
Greenwich Mean Time (GMT) is used from late Oct to late Mar, after which time the clocks go forward 1 hr to British Summer Time (BST).

Tipping
Tipping in England is at the customer's discretion. In a restaurant you should leave a tip of 10-15% if you are satisfied with the service. If the bill already includes a service charge, which is likely if you are in a large group, you needn't add a further tip. Tipping is not normal in pubs or bars. Taxi drivers may expect a tip for longer journeys, usually around 10%.

Tourist information
Tourist information centres (TICs) can be found in most towns. Their addresses, phone numbers and opening hours are listed in the relevant sections of this book. Opening hours vary depending on the time of year, and many of the smaller offices are closed or have limited opening hours during the winter months. All tourist offices provide information on accommodation, public transport, local attractions and restaurants, as well as selling books, local guides, maps and souvenirs. Many also have free street plans and leaflets describing local walks. They can also book accommodation for a small fee.

Museums, galleries and historic houses

Over 300 stately homes, gardens and countryside areas, are cared for by the **National Trust** ① *T0844-800 1895, www.nationaltrust.org.uk*. If you're going to be visiting several sights during your stay, then it's worth taking annual membership, which costs £53, £25 if you're aged under 26 and £70 for a family, giving free access to all National Trust properties. A similar organization is **English Heritage** ① *T0870-333 1181, www.english-heritage.org.uk*, which manages hundreds of ancient monuments and other sights around England, including Stonehenge, and focuses on restoration and preservation. Membership includes free admission to sites, and advance information on events, and costs £47 per adult to £82 per couple, under-19s free. **Natural England** ① *T0845-600 3078, www.naturalengland.org.uk*, is concerned with restoring and conserving the English countryside, and can give information on walks and events in the countryside.

Many other historic buildings are owned by local authorities, and admission is cheap, or in many cases free. Most municipal **art galleries** and **museums** are free, as well as most state-owned museums, particularly those in London and other large cities. Most fee-paying attractions give a discount or concession for senior citizens, the unemployed, full-time students and children under 16 (those under five are admitted free in most places). Proof of age or status must be shown.

Finding out more

The best way of finding out more information is to contact Visit England (aka the English Tourist Board), www.visitengland.com. Alternatively, you can contact VisitBritain, the organization responsible for tourism. Both organizations can provide a wealth of free literature and information such as maps, city guides and accommodation brochures. Travellers with special needs should also contact VisitEngland or their nearest VisitBritain office. If you want more detailed information on a particular area, contact the specific tourist boards; see in the main text for details.

Visas and immigration

Visa regulations are subject to change, so it is essential to check with your local British embassy, high commission or consulate before leaving home. Citizens of all European countries – except Albania, Bosnia Herzegovina, Kosovo, Macedonia, Moldova, Turkey, Serbia and all former Soviet republics (other than the Baltic states) – require only a passport to enter Britain and can generally stay for up to 3 months. Citizens of Australia, Canada, New Zealand, South Africa or the USA can stay for up to 6 months, providing they have a return ticket and sufficient funds to cover their stay. Citizens of most other countries require a visa from the commission or consular office in the country of application.

The UK Border Agency, www.ukba.homeoffice.gov.uk, is responsible for UK immigration matters and its website is a good place to start for anyone hoping visit, work, study or emigrate to the UK. For visa extensions also contact the UK Border Agency via the website. Citizens of Australia, Canada, New Zealand, South Africa or the USA wishing to stay longer than 6 months will need an Entry Clearance Certificate from the British High Commission in their country. For more details, contact your nearest British embassy, consulate or high commission, or the Foreign and Commonwealth Office in London.

Weights and measures

Imperial and metric systems are both in use. Distances on roads are measured in miles and yards, drinks poured in pints and gills, but generally, the metric system is used elsewhere.

Contents

Footprint features

Norfolk

Norfolk is the county that typifies East Anglia for most people: big skies, wide views over the flat land and hazy horizons. Now visitors have discovered the delights of this expansive rural backwater beside the North Sea, with its strange ways and watery light.

Norwich, the capital of the county, was the third richest city in England during the Middle Ages and today rivals York as the best-preserved medieval townscape beneath cathedral and castle in the land.

Great Yarmouth is Norfolk's top seaside resort, still one of the most spirited on England's east coast, and behind it lie the Broads, where pleasure-boating was born in the mid-19th century and is still going strong. These waterways winding through marshland and open lakes are busy all summer with motor cruisers and sailing boats as well as hiding more peaceful and secluded spots alive with rare water birds and also, much to the concern of the farmers, the coypu.

The jewel in Norfolk's holiday box of tricks is undoubtedly its north coast. From Blakeney to Brancaster, the seemingly limitless sandy beaches, salt marshes, tidal inlets and quiet fishing villages have won the hearts of London's second-homers who work in film and a particular ruminative breed of regular epicurean re-visitors.

Another unusual and much less well-known landscape can be found in Breckland, where acres of pine forest and scrub cover the sandy hills and heaths.

Norwich

Norwich, never loud or brash, is quietly confident of itself. Stranded in the middle of the flatlands of East Anglia, it is, as its inhabitants are fond of saying, a "fine city", a typically understated boast that is nonetheless borne out by the way in which the place manages to combine so many different layers of English history within the bustle of a busy provincial capital, set off by some bold forays into cutting-edge modernism. As recent excavations have shown, this bend in the River Wensum was used as a place of settlement in Bronze Age times and was subsequently occupied by successive waves of invading forces, from the Vikings and the Romans to – most significantly – the Normans, whose spectacular castle and cathedral still stand at the heart of the city. It is, though, entirely possible to tire of medieval churches – of which Norwich has a surfeit – the natural antidote to which is the Sainsbury Centre of Visual Arts, a latter-day temple to the new religion of modern art and a truly world-class museum. Norwich's churches are famously only outnumbered by the city's pubs, where a large student population ensures that the nightlife, while not desperately fashionable, is far from dull. Norwich also provides an ideal base for those interested in exploring Norfolk's many stunning beaches or the more discreet charm of the county's numerous villages and market towns.

Arriving in Norwich

Getting there Stansted International Airport, 85 miles away by road, is linked to Norwich by a **National Express** coach service, T08717-818178, www.national express.com. Norwich also has its own **airport**, T01603-411923; www.norwich airport.co.uk, a few miles to the north of the city, and a 20-minute taxi ride from Norwich centre. The park and ride bus, with a stop just a few minutes' walk from airport, runs buses to the city centre Monday to Saturday; see www.norfolk.gov.uk for timetable information. Alternatively, First buses (www.firstgroup.com) operate a service from Hellesdon, which is within walking distance of the airport. There are train services from direct from London Liverpool Street and other local towns and villages; for travel from the Midlands, the north or Scotland, change at Peterborough. The **drive** to Norwich from London, just over 100 miles, is likely to take you about three hours. Take the M11 as far as Cambridge and turn off onto the A11. The city contains a number of multi-storey and pay-and-display car parks, as well as some short-term parking spaces in the centre of town. The train station is a 10-minute walk from the centre. There are regular bus services into the city and a taxi rank is just outside the station. Coaches arrive at the bus station at Surrey Street, in the city centre. ▶▶ *See Transport, page 45.*

Getting around Norwich city centre is compact enough to make most places accessible by foot. The 25 bus links the centre with the train station and the 21 or 22 take you to B&B land to the west of the city. For the Sainsbury Centre, a few miles away on the University of East Anglia campus, take the 25, 25a or X25 from the city centre.

Tourist information The main tourist office ① *T01603-213999, tourism@ norwich.gov.uk, Millennium Plain, Mon-Sat 0930-1730, plus mid-Jul to mid-Sep Sun 1000-1500,* is on the ground floor of The Forum, the vast, hi-tech library and visitor centre on the southwest corner of the marketplace.

Norwich

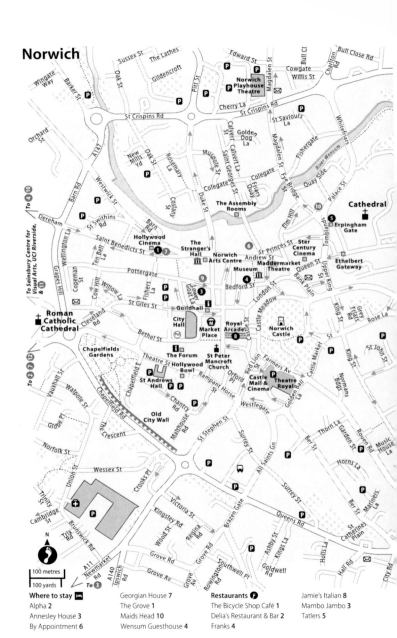

100 metres
100 yards

Where to stay
Alpha **2**
Annesley House **3**
By Appointment **6**

Georgian House **7**
The Grove **1**
Maids Head **10**
Wensum Guesthouse **4**

Restaurants
The Bicycle Shop Café **1**
Delia's Restaurant & Bar **2**
Franks **4**

Jamie's Italian **8**
Mambo Jambo **3**
Tatlers **5**

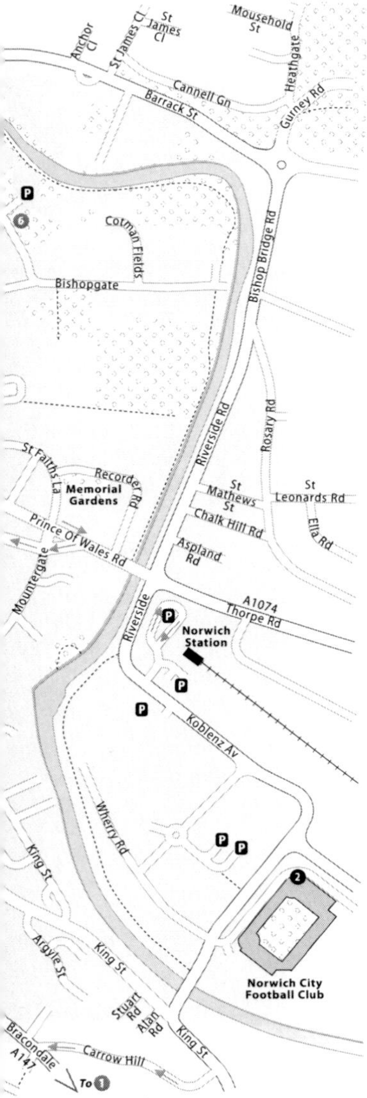

Map labels: Anchor, St James Cl, St James Cl, Mousehold St, Heathgate, Cannell Gn, Barrack St, Gurney Rd, Bishop Bridge Rd, Cotman Fields, Bishopgate, Riverside Rd, Rosary Rd, St Faiths La, Recorder Rd, Memorial Gardens, St Mathews St, St Leonards Rd, Ella Rd, Prince Of Wales Rd, Chalk Hill Rd, Mountergate, Aspland Rd, A1074 Thorpe Rd, Riverside, Norwich Station, Koblenz Av, Wherry Rd, King St, Argyle St, King St, Norwich City Football Club, Stuart Rd, Alan Rd, King St, Bracondale, Carrow Hill, A147, To

Pubs & bars
Adam & Eve **6**
Belgian Monk **9**
Fat Cat **10**
Garden House **11**
The Last Winebar **12**
Lounge **7**

Places in Norwich

Begin your tour where the city began, inappropriately enough at a place called Tombland, the original heart of Norwich. The **Erpingham Gate**, given to the city by the eponymous gent who led the English archers at Agincourt in 1420 and whose statue stands above the archway, acts as an entrance to the cathedral grounds. The impressive **cathedral** ① *T01603-218300, www.cathedral.org.uk, daily 0730-1800, free, visitor centre Mon-Sat 0930-1630, Sun 1200-1500*, itself was begun in 1096 and finally completed in 1278, though the roof and spire (96 m) date from the later medieval period, following a fire in 1463. Look under the bishop's throne, behind the high altar, for the remains of a more ancient Norfolk throne, symbolizing the continuity of local worship. A series of 255 painted bosses set high in the nave vaulting depict the entire Bible story, while other treasures include the exquisite carving around the prior's doorway leading onto the cloisters and the medieval paintings in St Luke's Chapel. There is also a shop, restaurant and café, labyrinth, herb garden and Japanese garden.

Leaving the second-hand bookshops of Tombland behind, walk up the hill into Upper King Street and then left into Castle Meadow for the castle. Perched high up on its grassy mound, **Norwich Castle** ① *T01603-493649, Jul-Sep Mon-Sat 1000-1700, Sun 1300-1700, closing at 1630 daily Oct-Jun, café and shop, £6.80, under-16s £4.90, special exhibitions £3.50, under-16s £2.60*, looks surprisingly modern for a Norman building, explained in part by the fact that it was resurfaced in the 19th century. Originally built as a royal palace, it subsequently became a prison, before its present incarnation as Norfolk's principal museum, offering a high-quality mix of history, archaeology, natural history and

Food-ball crazy

English football grounds are not the obvious places to find haute cuisine, but Carrow Road, home of Norwich City, is different. Nicknamed the Canaries for their bright yellow shirts, Norwich have a very famous Chairman in Delia Smith, doyen of TV celebrity chefs and saviour of many a Middle England dinner party. Delia, a lifelong Norwich City supporter, has taken to her role like a duck to plum sauce and gave up her TV work to concentrate on trying to guide her beloved Canaries back to the top flight. But if Norwich can't find the recipe for success on the football field, at least their fans can look forward to a superior half-time snack.

fine art, both old and new. Move freely between the Twinings Teapot Gallery, the Norwich School of Painters and a celebration of Boudica, the flame-haired local harridan who led the resistance against the Romans, featuring the world's only virtual-reality chariot ride. There is also a reconstruction of an Anglo-Saxon grave, locally found Viking treasures and new galleries exhibiting decorative arts, as well as the usual castle attractions of dungeons and battlements.

Back at the castle, stroll west down into Gentleman's Walk, leading onto the main market place, filled by an eye-catching patchwork of multicoloured awnings, where you can buy anything from jellied eels to a new dog lead. Behind you, for a more refined shopping experience, is the Art Nouveau **Royal Arcade**, containing a shop dedicated to one of Norwich's most famous exports, Colman's Mustard; see page 44. On the right is the flint-clad 15th-century **Guildhall**, while ahead of you is today's **City Hall**, an Art Deco Egyptian-style massif, guarded by two imperious Abyssinian lions. On the left of the square is **St Peter Mancroft**, the largest of the city's 31 medieval churches and a particular favourite of the 18th-century Methodist preacher and hymnist John Wesley. Soaring evermore heavenward, in the left-hand corner, is **The Forum** ① *The Forum, T01603-727950, www.theforumnorwich.co.uk, daily 0700-midnight, free*, Norwich's other modern giant, designed by Michael Hopkins and opened in 2001, is first and foremost the city's main public library, including an important archive dedicated to the American servicemen stationed in the area during the Second World War. The glass-fronted central atrium also has coffee bars and pizza restaurants, the tourist information centre and **Fusion** ① *Mon-Sat 1000-1500, free*, a digital gallery, the largest of its kind in Europe.

Passing the entrance to the city hall on your left, head up into Upper and Lower Goat Lane, leading into Pottergate and, further on, to St Benedict's Street to find a concentration of independent clothes shops and characterful bars and restaurants. The **Stranger's Hall** ① *Charing Cross, T01603-667229, Wed and Sat 1000-1600, closed late Dec to mid-Feb, £3.80, under-16s £2.10*, at the bottom of St Benedict's, is a medieval merchant's house now given over to an interesting museum of English domestic life from Tudor to Victorian times. Head straight on into Princes Street and make a left and right into **Elm Hill**, an atmospheric, cobbled street of timber-framed 16th-century merchants' houses, now home to shops selling crafts, second-hand books and antiques. If it's that time of day, this is also a good place to find a restorative cup of tea and a scone.

The **Sainsbury Centre for Visual Arts** ① *T01603-593199, www.scva.org.uk, Tue-Sun 1000-1700, free*, part of the University of East Anglia, is in Norman Foster's vast 1970s aircraft hangar and contains top-notch modern art, provocatively displayed alongside a wondrous hoard of objects gleaned from all parts of the space-time continuum, including Africa, America, ancient Egypt, the Pacific and medieval Europe. The contemporary collection is justly famous for works by Francis Bacon, Alberto Giacometti, Henry Moore, John Davies and Lucy Rie. The coffee bar, beside the main entrance and shop, is a good place to leaf through an arty purchase.

Lowestoft, Great Yarmouth and around

Although strictly speaking in Suffolk, Lowestoft almost joins up with Great Yarmouth in the north to form an urban coastal strip east of the Norfolk Broads. Both are ancient seafaring towns, although their fishing fleets are now a tiny fraction of the size that once made them rich. Sadly Lowestoft has the dilapidated air of a town that's down on its luck, but it still pulls in a considerable number of punters and young families in the summer months to enjoy its sandy beaches and seafront amusements. Great Yarmouth seems to have fared better than its southern neighbour during the post-war decline, thanks to the North Sea oil industry and also its more interesting situation on a peninsula of land formed by the river Yare as it sidles into the sea. Even busier during the summer, it claims to be Norfolk's most popular seaside resort and perhaps fancies itself as the Vegas of East Anglia.

Visiting Lowestoft and Great Yarmouth
Getting there Lowestoft is about 40 minutes from Norwich, and almost 1 hour and 30 minutes from Ipswich by slow stopping **trains** calling at Woodbridge, Wickham Market, Saxmundham, Halesworth and Beccles. Great Yarmouth is connected to Norwich (30 minutes away) by regular stopping trains. Lowestoft is the penultimate port of call for the A12, usually about a two hour 30 minute **drive** from London. Great Yarmouth is 9 miles further north, although reached more quickly from London along the dual-carriageway A47 via Norwich. ▸▸ *See Transport, page 46.*

Getting around Both Lowestoft and Great Yarmouth are easily navigated on foot and reliable bus services connect the towns. Exploring the Broads inland is best done by boat (see page 27) or bike and the countryside inland by car or bike.

Tourist information **Lowestoft TIC** ① *East Point Pavilion, Royal Plain T01502-533600, www.visit-sunrisecoast.co.uk, Mon-Fri 1030-1700, Sat 1000-1700.* **Great Yarmouth TIC** ① *Marine Parade, T01493-846346, www.great-yarmouth.co.uk, also at the Town Hall T01493-846345, Apr-Oct daily 0930-1730, Nov-Mar Mon-Fri 0930-1300 and 1400-1600.* **Broads Authority Information Centres** ① *visitor centres at Hoveton, How Hill and Whitlingham, www.enjoythebroads.com.* **Wells-next-the-Sea** ① *TIC Staithe St, T01328-710885, Mid-Mar to Oct Mon-Sat 1000-1700, Sun 1000-1600, Sep-Nov 1000-1400, Dec closed.*

Lowestoft
Sadly there's not much to keep visitors that long in Lowestoft unless it's busy beaches, a pier, fish and chips and family amusements you're looking for. That said, the old **harbour**

is worth exploring and the long esplanade still conjures up memories of the town's glory days despite heavy bombing during the war. The older part of town lies north of the harbour and Lake Lothing, the mouth of the river Waveney after it has expanded into Oulton Broad. Whapload Road runs past the massive Bird's Eye fish finger factory near the **Ness**, the most easterly point in the British Isles, and also past the **Lowestoft Maritime Museum** ① *T01502-561963, www.lowestoftmaritimemuseum.org.uk, Easter-Oct daily 1000-1700 (last admission 1600), £2, under-16s 50p*. This sweet little museum in the Sparrow's Nest in a park below the lighthouse is packed with models of boats and a mock-up of a trawler's cabin. The last deep-sea beam trawlers to fish out of Lowestoft were decommissioned in August 2002, bringing the town's 600-year fishing history to a close. Back by the harbour, the **East Point Pavilion**, a strange mock-Edwardian glass construction, is the centre of the boardwalk action, overlooking a big and busy sandy Blue Flag beach.

Great Yarmouth

Nine miles north of Lowestoft, Great Yarmouth was one of the wealthiest towns in East Anglia during the Middle Ages thanks to its control of the seaport for the inland waterway system leading to Norwich. Substantial sections of its old town walls, built between 1261 and 1400, have been carefully preserved and restored, although like its southern neighbour, much of the rest of the town was flattened by bombing in 1942. It sits on a long sandy promontory south of the harbourside train station that proved vital to the town's prosperity during the Victorian herring boom. This situation is what gives the place its dubious charm, a combination of quiet old riverside quays and full-on seaside resort. Nowadays the town does just well enough for itself thanks to the North Sea oil industry and tourism, drawing in crowds of fun-seekers during the summer. They usually make straight for **Marine Parade** and the beach. Along its seafront in high season, Great Yarmouth makes a tremendously tacky neon-lit spectacle of itself: horse-drawn carriages ply the prom, fairground rides pump up the volume and its two piers, Britannia and Wellington, buzz with arcade amusements and slot-machine activity. Even in winter, this scene doesn't quite let up entirely.

The calmer inland face of the town is South Quay, with its famous **rows**, little alleyways running like a ladder down from the impressive **Church of St Nicholas** with its wide west front and nave, the largest of any parish church in England. Gutted by fire during the war, it was restored in Victorian style in 1962. Three 17th-century houses in **Row 111** ① *South Quay, T01493-857900, www.english-heritage.org.uk, Apr-Sep daily, by guided tour only at 1000, 1200, 1400 and 1600, £4.20, under-16s £2.50*, along with the Old Merchant's House, have been restored by English Heritage, with plasterwork ceilings and oak panelling. South of the Market Place, where stands the cute little **Fisherman's Hospital**, built as almhouses for old seadogs in 1702, surrounded now by the town's main shopping area, the redundant **quayside** has been redeveloped as a heritage attraction, including the **Nelson Museum** ① *26 South Quay, T01493-850698, www.nelson-museum.co.uk, Apr-Sep Mon-Fri 1000-1700, Sat-Sun 1400-1700, Feb-Nov 1000-1600, Sat-Sun 1300-1600, £3.50, under-16s £2*, featuring the Ben Burgess Nelson Memorabilia Collection of paintings and things connected to the one-armed and one-eyed naval hero. At No 4 South Quay, the **Elizabethan House Museum** ① *T01493-855746, www.nationaltrust.org.uk, Apr-Oct Mon-Fri 1000-1700, Sat-Sun 1200-1600, £3.90, under-16s £2*, has been restored to give some idea of life in Tudor times as well as the Conspiracy Room, where the downfall of Charles I was supposedly plotted, and some Victorian kitchens. Tucked behind South Quay is **The Tolhouse Museum** ① *Tolhouse St, T01493-858900, Apr-Oct Mon-Fri 1000-1700, Sat-Sun 1315-1700, £3.50, under-16s £2, including a free audio guide*, one of the oldest civic buildings in the country with medieval cells beneath and displays on crime and punishment down the ages.

There is a multi-million pound **Time & Tide Museum** ① *T01493-743930, Apr-Oct daily 1000-1700, Nov-Mar Mon-Fri 1000-1600, Sat-Sun 1200-1600, £4.90, under-16s £3.60*, on the herring industry and Yarmouth local history in the Tower Curing Works on Blackfriars Road. It also holds regular art exhibitions and has a shop, children's playground and a café with an outdoor terrace. Great Yarmouth's **Northwest Tower** is a medieval tower on the North Quay beside the Bure, built in 1344 as part of the town walls. **Great Yarmouth Potteries** ①, *18 Trinity Pl, off Blackfriars Rd, T01493-850585, www.greatyarmouth potteries.co.uk, Mon-Fri 0930-1600*, is a working pottery and also includes an interesting herring museum, detailing the history of the herring fishing and smoking industry in Great Yarmouth. North of the centre of town, back by the sea, the RSPB reserve at **North Denes Beach** provides room for a breeding colony of rare little terns, visible simply nesting on the sand from May to August.

Scroby Sands ① *www.eon-uk.com*, is an offshore wind farm generating enough electricity to power 30,000 homes. In Great Yarmouth is the **visitor centre** ① *North Drive, Esplanade, 01493-854608, end of May-Oct daily 1000-1600, free*, which has information on renewable energy, or you can visit the wind farm itself on a boat trip from Southwold, see page 45.

Around Beccles and Bungay

Seven and 14 miles inland from Lowestoft up the river Waveney respectively, Beccles and Bungay are two quaint old market riverside towns that compete with each other for the passing tourist trade to the southern Broads. Beccles boasts a busy **quayside** on the river. Also just in Suffolk, Bungay was rebuilt in Georgian style after a disastrous fire in 1688, sitting in a loop of the river commanded by the ruins of Baron Roger Bigod's 13th-century castle. South of Bungay, a medieval moated manor house makes a pleasingly antique setting for some top-notch real ales, at **St Peter's Brewery and St Peter's Hall** ① *St Peter South Elmham, near Bungay, T01986-782322, www.stpetersbrewery.co.uk, brewery tours Easter to Dec Sat and Sun every hour on the hour from 1100 until 1500, £5*. See also Restaurants, page 41.

Between these towns, to the north, a couple of miles up the A146 towards Norwich, are a few places well worth seeking out. **Hales Hall Barn** is a wonder: 55 m long, a thatched brick-built barn constructed in 1480 with defensive loopholes in its walls and stepped gables, standing beside a lawn in front of the old Tudor hall. It's the largest and most spectacular thatched barn in Norfolk, approached across Hales Green, a large wildflower-strewn piece of common. Sitting quietly in a meadow nearby, **St Margaret Hales** is an adorable thatched pre-Gothic church with a flint tower and sparse interior maintained by Redenham Church fund. Nearby are the attractive **Raveningham Gardens** ① *T01508-548152, www.raveningham.com, Easter-Aug, Thu 1100-1600, Sun, bank holidays 1400-1700, £4, under-16s free*, with its proper ha-ha and beautifully renovated walled garden.

Natural born cullers

It was a relatively short affair and it ended acrimoniously. The coypu, a huge South America rodent the size of a sheep, was introduced to Norfolk in 1929 and bred for its pelt, known to the fur trade as nutria, and fashionable at the time. By the outbreak of war there were some 3000 being farmed for fur but a great flood in the 1940s enabled them to escape from their enclosures. They soon spread along a tributary of the Yare and then to the Broads. In no time at all they had settled happily into the East Anglian countryside. Numbers were initially limited by the demand for pelts but when nutria went out of fashion the population spiralled out of control to an estimated 200,000 by the late 1950s. The coypu were now seen by the government as a serious threat to riverbanks and crops, particularly sugar beet and carrots. The Coypu Clearance Campaign for East Anglia was quickly followed by the ominous-sounding Operation Broadland as tens of thousands of the prolific little breeders were culled. The Ministry of Agriculture pumped millions into its coypu control centre and by 1990 announced it was ending its field checks. The war was won.

Four miles inland between Lowestoft and Great Yarmouth is the very grand Victorian industrialist's residence **Somerleyton Hall** ① *T01502-734901, www.somerleyton.co.uk, Apr-Sep Tue, Thu, Sun, bank holidays (also Wed in Jul and Aug) 1000-1700, house and gardens £9.95, under-16s £4.95, gardens only £5.95, under-16s £3.95.* There's not that much to see inside, visitors being restricted to the ground floor only, passing through the dining room and library, although the carved entrance hall with two large stuffed polar bears and an impressive hat collection is worth a look. Outside it's the yew maze, immense walled garden with extraordinary old greenhouses, loggia, and superb mature trees that are the real draw.

The Broads

Norfolk's most popular tourist destination, very busy in summer, and also one of Europe's most important wetland habitats, the Broads are made up of about 127 miles-worth of shallow but navigable waterways twisting through reedbeds and marshland, the flat landscape dotted with ruined windmills, occasionally opening out into wider lakes – the 'broads' themselves. The whole area is the main place that the British love to mess about in boats. Five rivers provide the water as they make their way east across the county to the sea at Great Yarmouth: the Waveney is the most southerly, creating the county's border with Suffolk as it flows in via Bungay and Beccles; the Yare comes in from Norwich; the Bure from Aylsham, joined by the Ant and Thurne near Ranworth. Clearly this strange and usually peaceful landscape can only really be appreciated and explored by boat. The sheer number of motor cruisers that ply the channels in high season once came close to ruining the peace they seek but steps have been taken in recent years to limit their use. The most picturesque craft still in use on these waters are the Norfolk wherries, their tall masts and sails gliding quietly through the flat landscape.

Visiting the Broads

Getting there The main **road** access points to the Broads are at Norwich, Loddon, and Lowestoft (for the southern section) and at Great Yarmouth, Wroxham, Horning, Stalham and Potter Heigham (for the northern section). Broadland villages that give some idea of the area's charm and can be reached by car include Rockland St Mary in the south, and Ranworth, Horsey and Woodbastwick in the north. Details of local **bus** services (few and far between) can be found out from **Traveline East Anglia** (T0871-200 2233, www.travelineeastanglia.org.uk). The Broads can be reached by fairly regular **rail** services within an hour from Norwich, with stations at Reedham, Wroxham and Acle and also to Berney Arms which has no road. There is also a narrow gauge railway, the **Bure Valley Railway** ① *T01263-733858, www.bvrw.com*, between Hoveton/Wroxham and Aylsham.

Getting around Most obviously by **boat**, although the Broads can also be very enjoyably explored on foot and by bike. A **cycleway** and footpath runs alongside the Bure Valley Railway; see under Getting there above. Hire bikes from **Broadland Cycle Hire** (**www.broadlandcyclehire.co.uk**), on the A1062 between Hoveton and Horning. One of the best boatyards on the Broads is **Martham Boats** (T01493-740249, www.marthamboats.com), in Martham on the outer reaches of the northern broads. They have a variety of traditional wooden sailing and also wooden motor boats which they build themselves, also available for day hire. **Hoseason's** (T0844-847 1356, www.hoseasons.co.uk) are the big commercial operators in the area.

Tourist information Hoveton/Wroxham TIC ① *Station Rd, T01603-782281*. **Ranworth TIC** ① *The Staithe, T01603-270453*. **Broads Authority Information Line** ① *www.enjoythebroads.com*. **Broads Authority Information Centres** ① *Hoveton, How Hill and Whitlingham.*

Orientation The area divides neatly into northern and southern navigations: the former, based on the Bure, Ant and Thurne being the more popular and the most scenic (all the rivers are more attractive in their upper reaches) and with more of the broads themselves. These reed-fringed lagoons were created by peat-cuttings started in the 13th century which have slowly flooded over the years. They vary in size from small pools to the largest expanse at Hickling Broad. There are 63 of them altogether, mostly in the northern area. Thirteen are open for boating all year, as well as the navigable channels on Martham and Sutton Broads, and Womack Water. Two more, Black Horse Broad and Horsey Mere, are open during the spring and summer. All have been damaged by agribusiness and pleasure boating. Work has been done to restore Cockshoot and Barton Broads to their 1930s condition, involving the reduction of the phosphate concentration in the rivers. (Barton Broad is where Nelson learnt to sail.) Wind-powered mills in varying states of dilapidation can be seen all over the Broads, although only one (the restored Clayrack drainage Mill at How Hill) is still used to drain marshland, while several others (Herringfleet, Thurne Dyke, Berney Arms (see below), Horsey and Stracey Arms) have also been restored, some by the Norfolk Windmills Trust. Some of these mills are open to the public as part of National Mills Weekend in May (11-12 May 2013); see www.nationalmillsweekend.co.uk.

Southern Broads

Breydon Water is the large 800 ha tidal lake next to Great Yarmouth, with glistening mudflats at low tide, fed by the rivers Yare and Waveney. Four miles up the Yare, **Berney Arms** boasts its own request-stop on the railway, no road, and the tallest drainage **windmill** ① *www.english-heritage.org.uk, T01493-857900, access is for pre-booked groups only or visit on National Mills Weekend, see above*, in the UK with magnificent views over Breydon Water and the surrounding marshland from the top. It stopped pumping water as recently as 1951. Apart from the train, you can access the windmill by walking 6 miles from Great Yarmouth or 3 miles from Halvergate.

Berney Marshes and Breydon Water RSPB Nature Reserve ① *www.rspb.org.uk*, includes the Halvergate Marshes and is teeming with waders and wildfowl. It's a pleasant walk from the villages of either Halvergate or **Reedham**, where a chain ferry for cars crosses the river and there's a swinging railway bridge. A couple of miles upstream, the Hardley Cross obelisk marks the boundary between the navigational jurisdiction of Great Yarmouth and Norwich, near the mouth of the twisting river Chet, flowing in the three miles or so from **Loddon**. This little 18th-century market town is a good alternative to Yarmouth or Lowestoft for boat hire. Its Holy Trinity Church dates from 1490, with a fine hammer-beam roof, and also a panel on the rood screen depicting William of Norwich, a 12th century boy martyr, and a very old almsbox.

The largest stretch of open water in the Yare valley is nearby at **Rockland Broad**, where day boats can be hired and there's a decent pub in Rockland St Mary. **Surlingham Broad**, at Brundall, has a Swallows-and-Amazons style maze of little channels connecting its two lakes. Seven miles or so further upstream stands Norwich, the centre of which can be reached along the river Wensum.

Following the river Waveney upstream from Breydon Water passes **Burgh Castle** (open any reasonable time) where the impressive remains of a walled third-century Roman fort overlook the river. Five miles further the river is bridged at **St Olave's**, a small single-street 17th-century village named after the patron saint of Norway. The ruins of its 13th-century Augustinian priory stand too close to the busy A143 for comfort. The river runs on into **Oulton Broad** and Lowestoft passing close to Somerleyton Hall (see page 26) and bends round beneath Burgh St Peter, with its thatched church. Seven miles further on is the dignified old town of Beccles (see page 25), from where the river's most beautiful reaches run past **Geldeston Lock** where there's an atmospheric old pub (see page 43).

Northern Broads

The Bure enters Great Yarmouth from the north after an unattractive and congested three-mile stretch of the river below Stokesby. Five miles further upstream, the Bure comes into its own as it's joined by the Thurne, which has run south for three miles from **Potter Heigham**. A boat hire centre second only to Wroxham, Potter Heigham has an entertainingly difficult medieval bridge to navigate, where larger boats are required to take on a pilot to shoot the central arch at full speed. Southwest of the town, near Ludham, is **Toad Hole Cottage** ① *Electric Eel, How Hill, T01692-678763, Apr, May and Oct Mon-Fri 1030-1300 and 1330-1700, Sat-Sun 1030-1700, Jun-Sep daily 0930-1700, free*, an old eel catcher's cottage that conjures the atmosphere of Victorian country living and also runs quiet 50-minute **boat trips** ① *Apr-Oct on the hour every hour 1000-1700 Apr, May, Oct* *weekends only 1100-1500, £4.50, under-16s £3.50,* through fen and reed swamp on the river Ant aboard the *Electric Eel*.

Further up the Thurne, the sea feels very close. **Hickling Broad**, the largest of the Broads, is owned by the Norfolk Wildlife Trust, and comes closest to most people's idea of a typical broadland scene. Nature trails start from the **Pleasure Boat Inn** (www.thepleasureboat.com), heading round the lake on boardwalks and dry land. A narrow channel leads into **Horsey Mere**, another secluded lake, owned by the National Trust and overlooked by their **Horsey Windpump** ① *www.nationaltrust.org.uk, T01263-740241, Mar Sat-Sun 1000-1630, Apr-Oct daily 1000-1630 (last admission 1630), £2.50, children £1,* restored following lightning damage in 1943. Expect to see the relatively rare swallowtail butterflies here in summer.

Back on the Bure at the mouth of the Thurne stands a well-preserved white **Thurne Dyke Drainage Mill** ① *T01692-672155, www.norfolkwindmills.co.uk, Easter-Aug 2nd and 4th Sun 1400-1600,* owned by Norfolk Windmills, from where a beautiful two-mile walk leads up to the picturesque ruins of **St Benet's Abbey**. These are the remains of the only religious house in Norfolk founded before the Norman Conquest, by King Canute, enclosed with a wall and battlements in 1327. It was also reputed to be the only religious house in England not actually dissolved by Henry VIII, and the Bishops of Norwich have remained Abbots to the present day. The Bishop arrives by wherry and preaches at the annual service on the first Sunday in August. In the 18th century a windmill was built in the ruins, its battered stump remains, and a cross of oak from the Royal Estate at Sandringham was erected on the site of the High Altar in 1987.

The best way to reach the Abbey is by hiring a boat at **Horning**, beyond the mouth of the river Ant. The route passes the entrance to **Ranworth Broad**, where the delightful broad-side village of **Ranworth** (which can also be reached by car) is blessed with a **church**, dating from 1370, containing an outstanding medieval painted screen. There's also an antiphoner book of 285 sheepskin pages with versicles and responses for the seven services for every day of the year illuminated with exquisite lettering. There are superb views over broadland from the top of its tower. **Ranworth Conservation Centre** is a floating information centre run by the Norfolk Wildlife Trust at the end of a boardwalk through woodland and fen habitats, dealing with the creation of the broads, their wildlife and conservation.

Five miles northwest of Ranworth, further up the Bure, **Wroxham** is the capital of the Broads sitting next to its 45-ha lake. The town is almost completely overrun with boaties, tourists and geese during summer, and the broad itself crammed with sailing dinghies. It's a reasonably good value place to hire a boat for the day though and also pick up picnic provisions. The **Bure Valley Railway** ① *Norwich Rd, Aylsham, T01263-733858, www.bvrw.co.uk, daily Apr-Oct, with limited services for the rest of the year, £8, under-16s £5, unlimited travel Rover tickets/returns £12.50, under-16s £6.50,* a narrow-gauge railway, built in 1990, runs the 9-mile, 45-minute trip from Wroxham to Aylsham via Coltishall, Buxton and Brampton. Nearby, **Hoveton Great Broad Nature Trail** was laid out in 1968, the first nature trail to be established in the region. With excellent views of Hoveton Great Broad, its adjoining fens and alder woodland, it can only be reached by boat. Moorings are available on the north bank of the Bure opposite Salhouse Broad.

Near Hoveton is **BeWILDerwood** ① *on the A1062 between Hoveton and Horning, www.bewilderwood.co.uk, Feb half term to Oct half term daily 1000-1730, 105-250 cm tall*

£12.50, 92-105 cm £10.50, under 92 cm free, a huge, quirky adventure park set in woodland featuring treehouses, zip wires, den building and imaginative creatures with names like Swampy and Mildred the Crocklebog.

North Walsham and **Stalham** are at the furthest northern tip of the Broads. At Stalham Staithe, the waterside **Museum of the Broads** ① *www.museumofthebroads.org.uk, late Apr-Sep daily 1030-1700, £5, under-16s £2.50*, has several buildings housing a variety of boat-related exhibits and displays on traditional Broadland industries.

North coast from Cromer to King's Lynn

Beyond Cromer, the crumbling cliff-top seaside resort in Norfolk's northeast corner, a really superb coast road wends west towards King's Lynn. It travels through a strange but no longer undiscovered seashore, half land and half sea, made up of shifting sands, shallow tidal inlets and wide stretches of salt marshes alive with waders, seabirds and geese. On the way, it takes in precious, small, one-time ports like Cley-next-the-Sea and Blakeney and the dilapidated dignity of Wells-next-the-Sea, its beach now more than a mile away. Holkham beach nearby must be one of the most beautiful in England, where the Household Cavalry sends its thoroughbreds for rest cures and partially owned by the very grand estate of the Earls of Leicester at Holkham Hall. A little inland, Felbrigg is another extraordinary country house, much more homely, while the Queen's modest retreat at Sandringham also draws in punters during the summer.

Visiting the north coast from Cromer to King's Lynn
Getting there Cromer and Sheringham are on a branch line run by **Greater Anglia** (T0845-600 7245, www.greateranglia.co.uk), from Norwich with the **Bittern Line** (www.bitternline.com) community railway. A Bittern rover (£7.80) covers unlimited travel on the Bittern Line and the Coasthopper bus (see below). The A149 is the main coast road, about three hours from London starting at either end. To explore the coast by **bus**, take the **Coasthopper** (T01553-776980, www.coasthopper.co.uk), which runs almost all the way along the A149, from King's Lynn to Sheringham.

Getting around Although the Coasthopper bus and rail to Cromer make this coast perfectly accessible without a car, many of the more surprising and secluded sights inland can only be reached with by car. See also www.travelineeastanglia.org.uk for all public transport options.

Tourist information Wells-next-the-Sea TIC ① *Staithe St, T01328-710885, wellsinfo@ north-norfolk.gov.uk, mid-Mar to Oct Mon-Sat 1000-1700, Sun 1000-1600, Sep-Nov 1000-1400, Dec-Jan closed*. **Walsingham TIC** ① *Shire Hall Museum, T01328-820510, Easter-Oct daily 1000-1600*, has very cheery staff.

North of the Broads
North of Great Yarmouth, the coastline curves round in one continuous beach all the way to Cromer and Sheringham. It has little to recommend itself to holidaymakers though, being not much good for swimming (dangerous in many places) and lashed by biting winds. Even so, the coast road has a certain breezy charm, dipping in and out of the sea

view, especially beyond the tiny village of **Happisburgh** (pronounced Hazebrugh by the locals), in the news in recent years due to rapid coastal erosion, which has left some houses dangerously close to the cliff edge. It's worth stopping here for a look into the church, and climbing the tower if it's open to look out to sea and over the Broads. The village also has a red and white striped lighthouse, caravan park and a good solid country pub, the **Hill House**, see page 43.

Cromer

The first town of any size, more than 30 miles from Great Yarmouth, is faded, sun-bleached Cromer. Standing on an impressive cliff, overlooking its long pleasure pier braving the steady ranks of breakers, the place was once quite grand. Dominated by a church with the tallest tower in the county, large Edwardian buildings line the cliff-top promenade, but the prevailing atmosphere is forlorn and unloved. The reek of greasy fish and chips stubbornly defies the sea breezes, though this is a top spot for local crab. **Bob Davies Crab Shop** at the end of Brunswick Terrace, and the **Lifeboat Café** near where all the crab-boats pull up on the slipway, are both reasonable bets for fresh crustacea. The **Cromer Museum** ① *T01263-513543, Apr-Oct Mon-Fri 1000-1600, Sat 1200-1600, Sun 1300-1600, closed Sun Nov-Mar, £3.50, under-16s £2*, in a former fisherman's cottage next to the church has been converted into a little local history museum, with some great photos of early 20th-century Cromer by North Norfolk photographer Olive Edis. Meanwhile the show gamely goes on at the **Cromer Pier and Pavilion Theatre** ① *T01263-512495, www.cromer-pier.com, performances late Jun-Sep.*

Inland from Cromer

A mile or so inland to the south, **Felbrigg Hall** ① *T01263-837444, www.national trust.org.uk, Mar-Nov Sat-Wed 1100-1700, summer school holidays open daily, gardens, café and shop Nov to mid-Dec Thu-Sun 1100-1500, parkland open all year, £8.70, children £4.10,* is the well-preserved seat of a Norfolk country gentleman that has been left as it was when given to the National Trust in 1969. Four generations of the Windham family's furniture, books and pictures fill the comfortable rooms almost as if it were still lived in, but its chief glory is architectural. The hall itself is best seen from the south west, to appreciate the startling change in style that took place over the course of the 17th century. The south front looks like a delightful little Jacobean house, built in 1620, while the west wing, added in the 1680s, represents one of the earliest examples of the handsome Italianate architectural style that came to dominate vernacular English buildings for over a century, and is now known as 'Georgian'. The kitchens have been restored and can now be visited, the walled garden has a thousand doves in the cote, and there's a pretty little church some distance away across the park.

Seven miles further inland, off the A140, stands probably the finest unmodified example of Jacobean architecture in the country, at **Blickling Estate** ① *Blickling, T01263-738030, www.nationaltrust.org.uk, house Feb half term daily 1100-1530, Mar-Nov daily except Tue 1200-1700, Nov to mid-Dec Sat-Sun 1100-1500, garden Jan to mid-Feb and Nov to mid-Dec Thu-Sun 1015-1600, mid-Feb to Nov daily 1015-1700, park and woodland open all year, £11.35, under-16s £5.65, gardens only £8.05, under-16s £4, 15 miles north of Norwich.* Built between 1610 and 1630, and probably designed by the same architect as Felbrigg, it's altogether a much more stately affair, little changed externally but revealing centuries of passing fashions and tastes inside. Highlights include the long gallery with its fabulous plasterwork ceiling, the Peter the Great Room designed to display a huge tapestry woven in 1764 of the mounted Tsar, given to Lord Buckinghamshire by Catherine the Great, and the surrounding parkland complete with a mile-long lake. The place is said to be haunted by the ghost of Anne Boleyn, who may have lived on this site as a child almost a century before the present house was built.

Five miles west of Blickling, a cluster of Norfolk villages are worth seeking out for their remarkable churches and unexpectedly cosy setting in this industrially farmed landscape. **Heydon** is a privately owned village that seems hardly to have changed in a couple of hundred years. The most recent construction was the well in commemoration of Queen Victoria's Jubilee in 1887. It clusters at gates leading to a jewel of an Elizabethan house, restored in the 1970s and set in a beautiful old park. A couple of miles away through thick hedges along tiny lanes, the village of **Salle** (pronounced Saul) boasts Norfolk's 'rural cathedral'. Apart from its sheer scale, evidence of the wealth that the cloth industry once brought to these parts, the church's interior contains remarkable carvings, including an angelic host supporting the chancel roof. Nearby, the church at **Cawston** has a mighty 15th-century tower, visible from miles around, and inside one of the best old hammer-beam roofs in the county. A mile or so to the west, near Reepham, the church at **Booton** is another matter entirely: it's the eccentric fantasy of a devout Victorian parson, displaying exuberant Gothic Revivalism dreamed up by Whitwell Elwin, an ascetic who was descended, like others around here, from the native American princess Pocahontas. He won the devotion of several rich young women who paid for the place and are commemorated in the windows of the nave as angels wandering through the fields.

Heading back towards the coast, **Baconsthorpe Castle** ① *www.english-heritage. org.uk, daily 1000-1600, free,* was built by local despot Sir John Heydon in the 15th century during the Wars of the Roses. Peaceful and substantial ruins beside a moat are all that remain, and are a good spot for a picnic. Beyond the old market town of Holt, **Letheringsett Watermill** ① *T01263-713153, www.letheringsettwatermill.co.uk, Whitsun-Sep Mon-Fri 1000-1700, Sat 0900-1300 (demonstrations 1330-1630), Oct-Whitsun Mon-Fri 0900-1600, Sat 0900-1300 (ring to confirm demonstration times), £3, under-16s £2, with demonstration £4 and £2.50,* is the county's last working flour-producing watermill, restored in 1982, with enthusiastic and knowledgeable volunteer millers. Three miles west of Holt, the **North Norfolk Steam Railway** ① *T01263-820800, www.nnrailway.co.uk, no services Jan-Feb except Feb half term,* runs 7 scenic miles from here to the coastal resort of **Sheringham** along 'the poppy line'. It shares its headquarters with the regular rail service's station at Sheringham, a sea-level imitation of Cromer, although the seafront has been badly disfigured by modern defences against coastal erosion.

Cley-next-the-Sea and Blakeney

The A149 coast road from Sheringham to Hunstanton, another 30 miles or so, ranks as one of the most delightful coastal routes in England. The North Sea is never more than a couple of miles away to the north, occasionally visible across gleaming mudflats or glistening salt marsh, sometimes hidden completely behind woods and sand hills, as the road rolls through a string of places called 'next-the-sea' that have long been left high and dry. Cley-next-the-Sea (pronounced 'Cly') is the first, an adorable little town and another that was once an important medieval port. Its church with its great south porch now looks

Walks on the Norfolk coast

- **Blakeney Point**: 6 miles there and back. Start: Cley Beach car park, a mile north of Cley-next-the-Sea. A challenging and strange walk along the Norfolk Coast's most spectacular shingle spit. OS Maps: Explorer 24, Landranger 133/132.
- **Holkham**: 2 miles there and back. Start: North entrance to Holkham Hall, A149. A walk through pine woods to marram grass dunes and an awesome sweep of shimmering sand. OS Maps: Explorer 24, Landranger 132.
- **Scolt Head Island**: 2 miles there and back. Start: Brancaster Staithe, 4 miles west of Burnham Market. Boat trip out to a national nature reserve and walks through sandy marshes. OS Maps: Explorer 23, Landranger 132.
- **Beacon Hill**: 3 miles there and back. Start: Beeston Regis, 3 miles west of Cromer. A gentle walk up to Norfolk's highest point around the aptly named Pretty Corner. OS Maps: Explorer 25, Landranger 133.

over a meadow instead of a harbour, and contains some extraordinary windows and medieval carvings in its nave. Potteries, cafés and restaurants line its old High Street and this is also the jumping off point for the long (5-mile), lovely walk out to **Blakeney Point Nature Reserve** ⓘ *Morston Quay, Quay Rd, Morston, T01263-740241, www.national trust.org.uk*. An easier option is to catch one of the grey seal-spotting boats that leave from Blakeney and Morston quaysides a few miles down the road, see page 45. Blakeney is a 3-mile sand and shingle spit enclosing saltmarshes and a harbour and a haven for wildlife.

One mile on from Cley, its medieval rival Blakeney also has an interesting **church**, belittling the harbour below, with an extra tower that was once believed to be a lighthouse. Apparently unlikely given that the main tower is taller, suggestions are now invited inside as to its true purpose. Another of the town's sights is the 14th-century cellar of a merchant's house called the **Blakeney Guildhall**. The village itself has the calm and unhurried air of a place dependent on the tides and several good overnight stops. Not surprisingly very popular (especially with birdwatchers) is the section of the **Norfolk Coast Path** leading through the salt marshes from here to Wells-next-the-Sea.

Stiffkey

Two miles beyond Morston, the path passes to seaward of Stiffkey (pronounced *Stewkey*), once famous for its mighty cockle women who lugged back huge bundles of the 'Stewkey blues' revealed on the mudflats at low tide. The village also once revelled in being the scene of a sobering Victorian morality tale about a philandering vicar who left the village in disgrace to become a lion tamer and was eaten. No such dramas today, but instead an almost ruined Elizabethan village hall, 15th-century brasses in the church and a very good pub called the **Red Lion**. Two miles deeper inland, at **Binham Priory** ⓘ *T01328-830362, www.english-heritage.org.uk, open any reasonable time*, are the extensive remains of a Benedictine priory, its great Norman nave still in use as the parish church, with a 13th-century west front that gets architectural historians going because it may have contained the earliest window tracery in the country.

Wells-next-the-Sea

Four miles down the road is the old town of Wells-next-the-Sea, not next the sea at all now, but nonetheless a fairly dignified, slightly down-at-heel seaside resort with a dinky little harbour, a cluster of rock shops and a sandy beach that's a mile's walk or narrow-gauge steam train ride from the quay, on the **Wells Harbour Railway** ⓘ *http://freespace.virgin.net/ michael.l/whr, runs mid-Mar to Oct half term at weekends then daily May-Sep 1030-1800, evening services during school and bank holidays, every 20 mins to the Pinewoods campsite*. The town itself is not a bad place to poke around for a while, browsing its small shops on Staithe Street or getting some chips on the quayside.

Little Walsingham

Probably still the most important pilgrimage shrines in the country, the most comparable thing to Lourdes on offer, is 4 miles south of Wells at Little Walsingham. Since the 11th century, Kings, Queens and commoners have made their way to Little Walsingham which these days caters for a wide variety of different denominations. The main two shrines are in the **High Anglican parish church** and in the **Roman Catholic Slipper Chapel**, with major pilgrimages to the former on the bank holiday Monday at the end of May, to the latter by Roman Catholic Mothers in late July, and an ecumenical pilgrimage to both in mid-August. All year the village is busy with believers. Unfortunately the vicar of Walsingham who established the Anglican shrine in the 1920s was 220 yards out in his estimation of the location of the original shrine which was set up in 1061 by the local lady of the manor, who had supposedly seen the Virgin Mary. Pilgrims from the sea can enjoy the last leg of their journey from Wells on the **Wells and Walsingham Light Railway** ⓘ *T01328-711630, www.wellswalsinghamrailway.co.uk, Apr-Oct, see website or call for timetables, journey time 30 mins, £8.50/7 return/single, under-16s £7/5.50*.

Holkham

Two miles west of Wells stands one of the most stately homes in England, the imposing neo-Palladian bulk of **Holkham Hall** ⓘ *T01328-710227, www.holkham.co.uk, late-Mar to Oct Mon, Thu and Sun 1200-1600, £12, under-16s £6, museum and gardens £7, under-16s £3.50, adventure playground only free*. This ponderous yellow brick-built palace, solidly Roman in inspiration, took over 30 years to complete, designed by William Kent who started work in 1734 for Thomas Coke. It's still inhabited today by his descendant the Earl of Leicester and both inside and out remains remarkably little altered since the 1770s, housing a great collection of old masters by the likes of Claude, Poussin and Rubens, powerfully evocative of the tastes of the time. There's also a Bygones Museum, with a History of Farming exhibition in honour of the family's great mid-19th-century agriculturalist and pioneer of seed improvement, Coke of Norfolk, a children's adventure playground set in woodland, and cafés and shops.

A mile's walk towards the sea from one of Holkham Hall's many gates leads through pine woods and sand dunes to **Holkham Beach**, a serious contender for the title of most spectacular beach in England and up there with the best in the world. At low tide, mile upon mile of shining sand stretches towards the horizon, the sea seeming to have vanished from view. It returns faster than a man can run, rolling in to lap or break on the wide expanse of tussocky dunes.

Burnham Market to Hunstanton

Four miles west of Holkham, a group of four villages called Burnham-something surround Burnham Market, a very smart Georgian town with plenty of antique shops and some good restaurants. **Burnham-Overy-Staithe** is the most picturesque of the villages, especially around its old creek. Further west, **Brancaster** is another charming place in a similar mould, but with better access to the sea and sandy beaches. After 6 more miles the road arrives at the seaside resort of **Hunstanton**, a marginally upmarket version of Cromer at the west end of the north Norfolk coast and milder in climate thanks to the fact that it faces west. Donkey rides, deck chairs, beach huts and rolled trousers are still just about in fashion here, alongside the usual amusement arcades and seaside tack overlooking the beach beneath the cliffs. Just south of the town, more than 100 different varieties of lavender are grown at the **Norfolk Lavender** ① *Caley Mill, Heacham T01485-570384, www.norfolk-lavender.co.uk, daily 1000-1700 (field tours mid-June until harvest), animal centre £3.50, under-16s £2.50*, some of their essences distilled and a 50-acre field of the purple scented stuff viewable by minibus. There's a fragrant plant centre and impressive herb garden too, as well as a small animal centre, children's play area and play barn. From July to August during harvest time you can also visit the distillery.

Sandringham and around

① *T01553-545408, www.sandringhamestate.co.uk, Easter-Oct daily 1100-1700, closed 27 Jul-2 Aug 2013. £12, under-16s £6, museum and gardens only £8, under-16s £4.50, Sandringham Country Park is open all year and is free.*

Eight miles south is Sandringham, the Queen's country house. Edward VII had the place built in 1870 when he was Prince of Wales as a very grand shooting lodge. It still comes across more like a very comfortable late-Victorian home than a royal palace. As well as tours of the house and gardens, there's a museum housing some Royal possessions, ranging from a 1900 Daimler to a half-scale Aston Martin that was used by Princes Harry and William.

Five miles east, 10 miles west of Fakenham, **Houghton Hall** ① *T01485-528569, www.houghtonhall.com, Mid-May to Sep Wed, Sun and bank holidays 1100-1700, exhibition and house £18, under-16s £10, gardens and grounds £8, under-16s £3, book in advance for exhibition tickets*, is a much more grand and beautiful affair, an 18th-century Palladian mansion designed by James Gibbs for Sir Robert Walpole, the first prime minister of Britain from 1721-42. He was the father of Horace, the Gothic novelist and Strawberry Hill arbiter of 18th-century taste, who apparently hated the place but is nonetheless buried in the church which was stripped of its village to make way for the park, the inhabitants being relocated in smart estate cottages a short distance away. The estate was later inherited by the first Marquess of Cholmondeley whose descendants still live here. In the grounds is a sculpture park, with works by Richard Long, among other artists, and a soldier museum, featuring the world's largest collection of model soldiers.

Five miles south of Sandringham, **Castle Rising** ① *on the A149, T01553-631330, www.castlerising.co.uk, Apr-Sep daily 1000-1800, Oct-Mar Wed-Sun 1000-1600, £4, under-16s £2.50*, is a remarkably well-preserved 12th-century domestic keep standing in the middle of mighty earthworks. It was once the palace and home of Isabella, dowager Queen of England.

King's Lynn

The castle stands near the outskirts of King's Lynn, once one of the most important seaports in the country. It suffered throughout the 20th century, during the Second World War and later at the hands of the developers, but is still an important local centre. The two towers of its church raise their heads above the mess, and beneath them can be found a remarkable Norman west front, and pockets of the town still looking much as it would have done in its heyday.

Swaffham and Breckland

Between Newmarket and Norwich, north of Bury St Edmunds, the thinly populated expanse of sand hills and heath called the Brecks comes as a distinct surprise in the chalk and wetland landscape of East Anglia. Never much use to farmers, in the last century whole tracts of the area were planted with eerie acres of conifers by the Forestry Commission to form Thetford Forest. The Ministry of Defence moved in too, appropriating training areas and establishing massive RAF and US airbases at Lakenheath and Mildenhall (in Suffolk). The combined effect could almost be described as Soviet. Even so, large areas have been set aside for ramblers along forest trails, and attractive stretches of the ancient Peddar's Way traverse the east of the region on its path up to the North Sea at Hunstanton. Unusually for the east of England, water is at a premium here: the only settlements of any size being clustered on the Little Ouse and Wissey rivers. Thetford, the birthplace of Thomas Paine, and Swaffham, with its Georgian dignity still intact, are the major market towns. Evidence of very early human industry can be explored near both at the Neolithic flint mines called Grimes Graves, and at Cockley Cley, where there's a funny little reconstruction of an Iceni village, popular with children. More recent architecture is beautifully represented at the medieval moated manor of Oxburgh Hall.

Visiting Swaffham and Breckland

Getting there Brandon and Thetford are on the Ely/Cambridge **train** line to Norwich (50 and 30 minutes, respectively). **National Rail Enquiries**, T08457-484950. Thetford is bypassed by the A11 **road** that runs up past Newmarket, about two hours (on a good day) from London. Swaffham is about 17 miles away up the A1065. For details of local **bus** services see the **Traveline East Anglia**, www.travelineeastanglia.co.uk.

Getting around Unfortunately a **car** is really the only practical way to access Breckland's more remote walking areas, although a cycle hired in Thetford would be a good alternative.

Tourist information Swaffham TIC ① *Market Pl, T01760-722255, www.around swaffham.co.uk, Feb-Dec Tue-Sat 1000-1600.* **Attleborough TIC** ① *Town Hall, Queen Sq, T01953-456930, Apr-Sep Mon-Sat 1000-1600, Oct-Mar Mon-Wed and Fri-Sat 1000-1400, Thu 1000-1600.* **Watton and Wayland** ① *The Dragonfly Visitor and Exhibition Centre, Wayland House, Watton, T01953-882058, www.wayland-tourism.org.uk, Easter-Sep Mon-Fri 1000-1600, Sat 1000-1300.*

Thetford and around

The largest centre of population in the area, Thetford is a quiet market town, peacefully situated on the banks of the rivers Little Ouse and Thet but disfigured by housing developments. Not much remains of its ancient roots apart from an Iron Age castle mound and the 14th-century gatehouse of Thetford Cluniac Priory, near the train station. The other thing worth looking at if you happen to be passing through is the **Ancient House** Museum ① *21 White Hart St, T01842-752599, Apr-Sep Mon-Sat 1000-1700, closing at 1600 Oct-Mar, £3.80, under-16s £2.10*, in a 15th-century timber-framed merchant's house. A local history museum with a small display on Thomas Paine who was born in the town and long disowned by the place for publishing his revolutionary *Rights of Man* in 1791.

Acre upon acre of pine wood stretches north and west of the town towards Brandon, straddling the Norfolk–Suffolk border, **Thetford Forest** ① *T01842-815434, www.forestry.gov.uk, £1.90 per hour parking fee for access to High Lodge Forest Centre*, planted in the 1920s by the Forestry Commission. It's a great area of walking or cycling (bike hire is also possible; call T01842-810090 to check availability), with lots of well-marked trails for all abilities. The High Lodge Forest Centre has an adventure playground, a sculpture trail and lots of other activities on offer. The tree top adventure trail, **Go Ape** ① *http://goape.co.uk, open Feb-Nov, weekends only in Mar and Nov, daily from the end of Mar-early Nov, prices start at £32, £16 for under-16s*, is also based in High Lodge. Afterwards, head to Elveden on the southern edge of Thetford Forest to refuel at the Elveden estate's restaurant or farm shop.

Seven miles to the northwest of Thetford Forest, well signposted, in a clearing in the trees near the middle of the forest, the strangely dimpled hillocks betray the presence of the best-preserved Neolithic flint mines in the country. Named **Grimes Graves** ① *www.english-heritage.org.uk, T01842-810656, Apr-Oct daily 1000-1800, Oct daily 1000-1700, £3.40, under-16s £2*, after the pagan god Grim, their 4000-year-old purpose was only understood in 1870. Visitors can descend 9 m underground by ladder down an excavated shaft to see how some of the material for the weapons and tools (reconstructed in the visitor centre) were extracted from the chalk. Flint-knapping demonstrations are occasionally given in the summer.

Seven miles to the northeast of Thetford, the local council has established the 8-mile **Great Eastern Pingo Trail** around the small village of Thompson. The route passes through some typical Breckland scenery where walkers are encouraged to spot pingos, the shallow depressions left in the ground by ice bubbles 20,000 years ago. The village itself is also a good leaping-off point for the **Peddar's Way**. This ancient pre-Roman track runs almost dead straight 30 miles from Knettishall Heath country park near Thetford to the Holme-next-the-Sea on Norfolk coast.

Swaffham

Swaffham, 14 miles north of Thetford, stands on the northern edge of the Breckland wilds. It has a spacious and unusual triangular **Market Place**, surrounded by elegant Georgian houses. Every Saturday a busy open-air market and public auction is held here beneath the Market Cross presented to the town by the Earl of Orford in 1783. Just off the Market Place is the Church of Peter and Paul, with a fine double hammer-beam roof. Just outside Swaffham (follow the signs from the centre) is the **EcoTech Centre** ① *Turbine Way, on the A47 near Swaffham, T01760-726100, www.ecotech.org.uk, Mon-Fri 1000-1600, free*, where you can climb a wind turbine for superb views, stroll in organic gardens and visit the heritage orchard. The turbine provides enough electricity to power a third of the homes in Swaffham. There's also a café here.

Two miles southwest of Swaffham, in the village of **Cockley Cley**, there's a fanciful little reconstruction of an **Iceni Village** ① *T01760-724588, www.icenivillage.com, Apr-Oct daily 1100-1730, opening at 1000 Jul-Aug, £6, under-16s £4,* from the days of Queen Boudicca. In fact it's more of a family villa than a village, but its attraction is boosted by the presence of an odd assortment of other features: the remains of a Saxon church found in a 17th-century farm cottage, a museum displaying farming tools and vehicles, a nature trail, lake and the somehow inevitable World War memorabilia exhibition.

Five miles further on the same road, **Oxburgh Hall** ① *(NT), T01366-328258, www.nationaltrust.org.uk, Apr-Oct Mon-Wed, Sat-Sun, 1100-1700, bank holidays and school holidays daily1100-1700, 5 Jan-22 Dec gardens only Sat-Sun 1100-1600, £8.10, under-16s £4.05, gardens only £4.50, under-16s £2.25, Nov-Dec free for gardens and tea room,* is a delightful medieval moated manor house. The Bedingfield family added the grand Tudor gatehouse in 1482 and their descendants still live here, amid rooms ranging from the gritty Middle Ages to cosy Victoriana, enhanced by an embroidery collection worked up by none other than Mary Queen of Scots herself.

Four miles north of Swaffham off the A1065, the **Peddar's Way** passes through the old village of **Castle Acre**, well worth a visit for its impressive remains of its **Castle Acre** Priory ① *the castle and bailey gate have unrestricted access,* and also the ruins of the **Castle Acre Priory** ① *Castle Acre, T01760-755394, www.english-heritage.org.uk, Apr-Sep 1000-1800, Oct 1000-1700, Nov-Mar Sat-Sun 1000-1600, £5.80, under-16s £3.50.* The splendour of this religious establishment in the 12th century can be appreciated from the elaborately decorated arch of its west front, which still stands and comes as quite a surprise in this remote spot. The 15th-century gatehouse, porch and prior's lodging are still habitable. There's also a modern herb garden on site demonstrating some of the medicinal plants the nuns might have used.

Norfolk listings

For hotel and restaurant price codes and other relevant information, see pages 9-12.

😊 Where to stay

Norwich *p19, map p20*

Accommodation is hard to come by bang in the middle of town and the majority of visitors to Norwich find themselves booking into a B&B in the area just west of the city centre down the Dereham and Earlham Rds.

£££ By Appointment, 25-29 St George's St, T01603-630730, www.byappointment norwich.co.uk. For something a little theatrical, this is a series of 3 merchant's houses dating from the 15th-century in the city centre, furnished with antiques and which includes a well-respected restaurant. Much of the fresh produce for the restaurant is supplied by the Victorian walled garden.

£££-££ The Grove, 59 Bracondale, T01603-622053, www.thegrove norwich.co.uk. Fifteen minutes' walk from the centre is this friendly 3-room B&B in a Victorian house, with large sash windows, antique fireplaces, bathrooms with rolltop baths and delicious home-made breakfasts.

££ Georgian House Hotel, 32 Unthank Rd, T01603-615655, www.georgian-hotel.co.uk. Opposite the Roman Catholic Cathedral, this is a family-run hotel within 5 mins' walk of the centre. Free Wi-Fi and parking.

££ Maids Head Hotel, in central Tombland, T01603-209955, www.maidshead hotel.co.uk. Opposite the Cathedral, this 13th-century hotel has well-decorated rooms, some with exposed wooden beams, and serves superb breakfasts.

££ Wensum Guesthouse, 225 Dereham Rd, T01603-621069, www.wensum guesthouse.co.uk. Modern rooms in a centrally located Georgian building. Free Wi-Fi and parking.

Lowestoft, Great Yarmouth and around *p23*

£££ Imperial, North Drive, Great Yarmouth, T01493-842000 www.imperial hotel.co.uk. The best smartish option in town, overlooking the prom at its northern end, with a reputable restaurant.

£££ Ivy House Country Hotel, Ivy La, Oulton Broad, Lowestoft T01502-501353, www.ivyhousecountryhotel.co.uk. A hotel set in 1.5 ha of attractive gardens and grounds, with large quiet rooms, surrounded by the countryside of the Broads.

££ Foxhole B&B, St Cross South Elmham, T01986-888180, www.foxcottage.org.uk. Pretty B&B in a quiet village 6 miles from Bungay, in Suffolk but close to the Norfolk border. Breakfast and other meals available using delicious home-grown, homemade and locally sourced ingredients.

££ Silverstone House, 29 Wellesley Rd, Great Yarmouth, T01493-844862. Five minutes' walk from the seafront, this is a clean and fairly comfortable B&B option.

The Broads *p26*

The best place to sleep on the Broads is on a boat. Other options are listed here.

£££ Norfolk Mead Hotel, Coltishall, T01603-737531, www.norfolkmead.co.uk. A Georgian manor housem which has become a discreet and sophisticated country house hotel, with individually furnished rooms and attractive grounds sloping down to the river Bure.

££ Fisherman's Return, Winterton-on-Sea, near Martham, T01493-393305, www.fishermans-return.com. Pub B&B close to a sandy beach in an out-of-the-way spot with good value bar food and 3 bedrooms.

££ Le Grys Barn, Wacton Common, near Long Stratton, T01508-531576, www.legrys-barn.co.uk. A beautiful 17th-century barn B&B decorated with Oriental rugs and antiques collected during the owner Julie's travels in Asia.

North coast from Cromer to King's Lynn
p30

££££ Blakeney Hotel, Blakeney, near Holt, T01263-740797, www.blakeney-hotel.co.uk. Straightforward and comfortable modern 4-star hotel on the quayside overlooking the marshes to Blakeney Point. Rooms are well appointed and most have views of the estuary or marshes. There's an indoor pool, steam room, sauna, a small gym and a billiard and games room. Friendly and efficient staff.

££££ Hoste Arms, The Green, Burnham Market, T01328-738777, www.thehoste.com. In the middle of Burnham Market, 2 miles from the beach, this is a good base for north Norfolk, especially Holkham and Wells. Rooms are spacious and quiet. This place thinks a lot of its kitchen and charges accordingly. Fresh local ingredients predominate on the extensive modern British menu. Part of **The Hoste** collection of places to stay in Burnham Market, which also includes **Vine House**, **Railway House** and 3 cottages.

££££ Morston Hall, Holt, 2 miles from Blakeney on the coast, T01263-741041, www.morstonhall.com. Small manor house with attractive rooms, a well-tended garden and award-winning top-quality restaurant, which has been given a Michelin star.

££££-£££ Cley Mill, Cley-next-the-Sea, T01263-740209, www.cleywindmill.co.uk. This is a remarkable converted windmill with wonderful marshland and sea views and very good food. The stables have been converted into self-catering accommodation or there is a sister cottage in Blakeney 2 miles away.

£££ Buckinghamshire Arms, Blickling, T01263-732133, bucksarms.co.uk. Comfortable rooms furnished with antiques in a 17th-century coaching inn with views of Blickling Hall. There's decent food too, served in the cosy bar and dining room, with a wood-burning stoves and works by local artists on the walls.

£££ The Gunton Arms, Cromer Rd, Thorpe Market, T01263-832010, www.theguntonarms.co.uk. Beautifully refurbished pub in a 400 ha deer park with individually decorated rooms, lots of modern art on the walls and a great restaurant (**££**), run by a former chef of Mark Hix. Recommended.

£££ The Pigs, Norwich Rd, Edgefield, Melton Constable, 3 miles from Holt, T01263-587634, www.thepigs.org.uk. Recently renovated family friendly pub with 10 well-appointed new rooms, some of which have their own saunas and courtyard with outdoor bath and firepit; marshmallows come with the room. Great play area for kids, designed by the people at BeWILDerwood treehouse adventure park (see page 29). Good food served in the bar too. Recommended.

£££ Saracen's Head, Wolterton, near Erpingham, T01263-768909, www.saracenshead-norfolk.co.uk. Hard to find but worth the effort, for this Georgian inn's superb food (booking advisable), real ales and cosy rooms with en suite bathrooms.

££ The King's Arms, Westgate St, Blakeney, T01263-740341, www.blakeney kingsarms.co.uk. Snug low-ceilinged old pub in 3 fishermen's cottages with cosy good-value little rooms and tempting fare on offer.

£ Sheringham YHA, 1 Cremer's Drift, T0845-371 9040 , www.yha.org.uk. A short walk from the train station and town centre.

Swaffham and Breckland *p36*

£££ Strattons, 4 Ash Close, Swaffham, T01760-723845, www.strattons-hotel.co.uk. Off the Market Square, a delightful and beautifully restored old Queen Anne house with individually decorated rooms above a rated restaurant. There's also a café deli selling local produce.

£££-££ Litcham Hall, Litcham, near King's Lynn, T01328-701389, www.litchamhall.co.uk. A very fine, elegant18th-century country house B&B set in 1.2 ha of beautifully kept gardens, with herbaceous borders, a walled garden and a pool.

£££-££ The Old Rectory, Ferry Rd, Oxborough, 8 miles southwest of Swaffham, T07769-687599, www.oldrectoryoxborough bandb.co.uk. B&B in a Georgian country house set in grounds with a pool, ruined 10th-century church, croquet lawn and a lake.

££ College Farm, Thompson, near Thetford, T01953-483318. B&B in a medieval former priest's house with a long history. Breakfast is served in the Jacobean dining room. Free Wi-Fi.

££ Old Red Lion, Castle Acre, T01760-755557, www.oldredlion.org.uk. Informal hospitality in this former pub, with a choice of double rooms or dormitories. They serve wholefood vegetarian meals only.

🍴 Restaurants

Norwich *p19, map p20*

££ Delia's Restaurant & Bar, Norwich City Football Club, T01603-218704, www.canarycatering.co.uk. Fri and Sat from 1900 till late or directly after a match, see the website. This is a place where you can combine an afternoon watching the beautiful game and an evening enjoying the recipes of TV chef Delia Smith, a director and majority shareholder of Norwich's first division football team, aka 'the Canaries'. The restaurant is inside one of the football ground's stands.

££ Jamie's Italian, 21-24 Royal Arcade, Castle St, T01603-519967, www.jamie oliver.com. The usual Jamie fare but it's a more spacious restaurant than some of his others and worth a visit for the beautiful building it's in.

££ Tatlers, 21 Tombland, T01603-766670, www.tatlersrestaurant.co.uk. Closed Sun. Probably Norwich's best-known restaurant, serving modern French-influenced dishes made with local produce in a chic yet homely setting.

££-£ Frank's Bar, 19 Bedford St, T01603-618902, www.franksbar.co.uk. Another great relaxed café, this time in the Lanes. It dishes up some great locally sourced food (including Brancaster mussels) with many vegetarian options and all day brunch on Sun. There is also a weekly film on Sun. Recommended.

£ The Bicycle Shop Café, 17 St Benedicts St, T01603-625777. Lovely little laid-back café with live music in the evenings. Recommended.

£ Mambo Jambo, 14 Lower Goat La, T01603-666802, www.mambojambo restaurant.co.uk. Offers good-value southern cooking – Creole, Cajun, Mexican – with an upbeat ambience.

£ Modern Life Café, Sainsbury Centre for Visual Arts, see page 22, www.scva.org.uk. Daily 0900-1700. Join history of art students in the Sainsbury Centre's licensed café overlooking the sculpture garden. There is a good value lunch (1200-1400), but it needs to be booked 24 hrs in advance.

Lowestoft, Great Yarmouth and around *p23*

£££-££ Seafood Restaurant, 85 North Quay, Great Yarmouth, T01493-856009, theseafood.co.uk. The only really good seafood restaurant in the town, offering the freshest fish and seafood, much of it caught locally. Friendly and efficient service.

££ St Peter's Brewery, St Peter South Elmham, near Bungay, T01986-782288, www.stpetersbrewery.co.uk. Closed Sun evenings and Mon. Good-value 2-course set lunch dishes and excellent real ales, including organic ales and fruit beer.

North coast from Cromer to King's Lynn *p30*

Apart from many of the places listed below, a variety of restaurants and pubs in the region are also very good at serving up fresh local produce in imaginative ways amid homely surroundings.

££ Byfords, Holt, T01263-711400, www.byfords.org.uk. Fantastic deli with lots of homemade goodies including delicious pastries and takeaway stone-baked pizza, as well as a great little café open from breakfast until dinner. It's also a self-proclaimed 'posh B&B' (**££**), if you fancy staying the night; it's the sister hotel of **The Pigs** in Edgefield nearby, see page 40.

££ The Crown Hotel, Buttlands, Wells-next-the-Sea, T01553-710209, www.thecrownhotelwells.co.uk. Modern British cooking of a very high standard in a former coaching inn, now a stylish hotel. The Crown Hotel is part of the Flying Kiwi Inns group of hotels and pubs in Norfolk, run by celebrity chef and New Zealander Chris Coubrough. Recommended.

££ Lifeboat Inn, Ship La, Thornham, T01485-512236, www.lifeboatinn thornham.com. Great food using local produce at reasonable rates in a rambling 16th-century inn a short walk from Brancaster beach. Owned by Marco Pierre White, the menu features lots of locally sourced ingredients, including Cromer crabs, King's Lynn shrimps and oysters and lobsters from Brancaster. The bar also offers the most welcoming fire on winter days.

££ The Red Lion, Stiffkey, T01328-830552, www.stiffkey.com. Excellent fresh local seafood, including delicious mussels, served in a hearty and unpretentious atmosphere, with a log fire roaring on cold days. Stiffkey beer on tap, along with other local ales.

££ The Salthouse Dun Cow, on A149 in Salthouse, between Blakeney and Cley, T01263-740467, salthouseduncow.com. Fantastic food and an original menu, featuring lots of locally sourced ingredients including beef from Salthouse marshes and mussels from nearby Morston. Recommended.

££-£ Three Horseshoes, Bridge St, Warham All Saints, T01328-710547. Hearty, good-value dishes including homemade pies using local produce at this no-frills atmospheric pub which serves some great Norfolk ales.

£ Cliff Top Café, Cliff Rd, Overstrand, T01263-579319. Closed in Jan. Delightful café in a plum spot overlooking the sea and offering wholesome inexpensive food and afternoon cream teas.

£ Holt Tea Rooms, Janoway House, Church St, Holt, 3 miles south of Kelling on the A149 coast road, T01263-713232. Homemade doughnuts are a speciality at these popular tea rooms and they also do delicious quiche.

Pubs, bars and clubs

Norwich *p19, map p20*

The Adam and Eve, 17 Bishopsgate, T01603-667423. Norwich's oldest pub, dating from the 13th century and with bags of character, in the shadow of the cathedral walls. Sit outside with your pint and admire the ivy. Great local ales and excellent food.

The Belgian Monk, 7 Pottergate, T01603-767222, www.thebelgianmonk.com. This pub allows you to complement your research into an unholy array of Belgian beers and with mussels and chips and other examples of robust gastronomie. The mussels come from Brancaster just up the road.

The Fat Cat, 49 West End St, off Dereham Rd, T01603-624364, www.fatcatpub.co.uk. This pub is beloved of real ale drinkers, stocking a huge range of barrelled beers (up to 30) and a good stock of the Belgian bottled variety too.

The Garden House, Pembroke Rd, off Earlham Rd, T01603-628059, www.gardenhousepub.co.uk. Like the Fat Cat, another pub in the so-called 'Golden Triangle' of student living. Very popular, with a huge garden and a menu featuring food from their own smoker.

The Last Wine Bar, 103 Unthank Rd, T01603-626626, www.lastwinebar.co.uk.

Housed in a former Victorian shoe factory, with some original features, and close to the Playhouse theatre, is this welcoming bar, which is also a restaurant. There is an extensive wine list.

Lounge, 13 St Benedicts, http://thelounge norwich.co.uk. This bar is from the school of cool, minimalist styling and ambient beats, offering a whole range of events, including salsa, comedy nights and poetry readings.

The Broads p474

Fur and Feather, Woodbastwick (between Ranworth and Wroxham), T01603-720003, http://thefurandfeatherinn.co.uk. Large pub that serves as the main outlet for the local award-winning Woodfordes brewery and also does reasonable food (**££**).

Horsey Nelson, Horsey, T01493-393378. An eccentric, unpretentious and cosy country pub, with a good choice of beers, close to the beach.

Locks Inn, Geldeston, between Beccles and Bungay, T01508-518414, www.geldestonlocks.co.uk. Beside the River Waveney but hidden away down a farmyard track, does decent pub grub, although it's the location, with a waterside beer garden, and interior of the old place that make it. Lots of live music, including folk on Thu evenings and music on Sat evenings and Sunday afternoons. You can catch Big Dog Ferry from the Lido in Beccles; see the pub website for details.

North coast from Cromer to King's Lynn p30

The Hill House, Happisburgh, T01692-650004. A characterful freehouse pub (once one of Arthur Conan Doyle's favourite haunts), in a quiet coastal village with great views over the Broads and out to sea.

Swaffham and Breckland p36

The Swan, Brandon Rd, Hilborough, T01760-756380, www.hilboroughswan.co.uk.

A good pub with huge open fires, beams and brickwork, real ales, bright and welcoming with reasonable food. Also has rooms available (**££**) and self-catering apartments.

● Entertainment

Norwich p19, map p20
Cinema
Norwich has 3 multiplex cinemas: **Hollywood Cinema** in Anglia Sq, T01603-621903, www.hollywoodcinemas.net; **Vue** in the Castle Mall shopping centre, T08712-240240, www.myvue.com; and the **Odeon** at Riverside Leisure Park, T0871-224 4007, www.odeon.co.uk.

Cinema City, St Andrews St, T0871-902 5724, www.picturehouses.co.uk. The art house cinema, in a historic building showing independent films and some blockbusters (it has 3D too). There's also a great bar and restaurant here, called The Dining Rooms (http://norwichdiningrooms.co.uk).

Theatre
The city is well served by theatres. It has 3 main theatres, the **Norwich Playhouse** in St George's St, T01603-612580, www.norwichplayhouse.co.uk; the **Theatre Royal** in Theatre St, T01603-630000, www.theatreroyalnorwich.co.uk, which is the city's largest theatre; and the more alternative **Maddermarket Theatre**, in St John's Alley, T01603-620917, www.maddermarket.co.uk. There is also the **Puppet Theatre**, St James, Whitefriars, T01603-629921, www.puppet theatre.co.uk, which holds puppet shows created by their own company as well as those by touring companies. It also has puppet-making workshops. The **Sewell Barn Theatre**, Constitution Hill, T01603-697248, www.sewellbarn.org.uk, is an amateur theatre company located in a small barn. The **Garage Theatre**, 14 Chapelfield North, T01603-283382, www.thegarage.org.uk, is a performing arts centre focusing on theatre

with young people, with regular performances.

Music
Classical concerts are held in **St Andrew's and Blackfriars' Halls**, T01603-628477, www.standrewshall.co.uk, and also in **The Assembly Rooms**, Theatre St, T01603-626402, www.assemblyhouse norwich.co.uk. There might also be something happening at the friendly **Norwich Arts Centre**, in St Benedicts St, T01603-660352, norwichartscentre.co.uk – Nirvana played here on their first UK tour to an audience of 87 people.

✿ Festivals

Norwich *p19, map p20*
The city is host to a variety of festivals throughout the year.
Feb-Jun **Spring Literary Festival** is held at the University of East Anglia, where the famous creative writing course, founded by Sir Malcolm Bradbury and Sir Angus Wilson, has been taught by a host of well-known writers including Angela Carter, Andrew Motion and Rose Tremain and has produced such luminaries as Anne Enright, Ian McEwan, Graham Swift and Kazuo Ishiguro.
May Norfolk and Norwich **Festival**www.nnfestival.org.uk. Lots of cultural events in the city, including music, dance and theatre performances.
Sep-Oct The **Norfolk Food Festival**, www.norfolkfoodfestival.co.uk. Loads of food-related events throughout the county with many taking place in Norwich.
Sep-Dec The **Autumn Literary Festival**, the same as its spring equivalent; see above.
Oct Norwich Beer Festival, www.norwichcamra.org.uk, in the last week of the month.

○ Shopping

Norwich *p19, map p20*
As well as all the usual big name brands in the Castle Mall shopping centre (www.castlemallnorwich.co.uk), the area around the cathedral harbours a few little surprises such as the **Colman's Mustard Shop**, 15 Royal Arcade, T01603-627889, www.mustardshopnorwich.co.uk. All things bright yellow and mustard-themed from the famous Norwich mustard manufacturers, including a museum. In the atmospheric cobbled alleys and streets of Norwich Lanes, Timberhill and Elm Hill are lots of independent shops, selling antiques, second-hand books and vintage clothes. The city's huge market is held Mon to Sat in front of City Hall.

North coast from Cromer to King's Lynn *p30*
The Cley Smokehouse, High St, Cley, T01263-740282, www.cleysmokehouse.com. Famously good for picnic materials like fresh-dressed crabs, home-made pâté, wild salmon, wild smoked salmon, anchovies and crayfish tails.
Made in Cley, High St, Cley, T01263-740134, www.madeincley.co.uk. An interesting shop selling lots of crafts, including pottery, jewellery, prints and sculpture.
Picnic Fare Delicatessen, Cley, T01263-740587, www.picnic-fayre.co.uk. A highly rated East Anglian food shop. Come and stock up on picnic goodies before you visit the beach.

▲ What to do

Norwich *p19, map p20*
Boat trips
City Boats, T01603-701701, www.cityboats.co.uk. Boat trips of 20 mins to 3¾ hrs are available departing daytime and

evening from Elm Hill Quay and Norwich Station Quay, from £4 single, under-16s £3.

Bowling
Hollywood Bowl, Wherry Rd, T0844-826 1466, www.hollywoodbowl.co.uk. 26 bowling lanes, with bar and food area. From £4.95, under-16s £3.95.

Tours
Blue Badge Guide, TIC, T01603-213993, tic@visitnorwich.co.uk. Walking tours lasting approximately 1 hr 30 mins departing from the tourist centre; £4, under-16s £1.50.
Norwich Ghost Walks, T07831-189985, www.ghostwalksnorwich.co.uk. To get thoroughly spooked, go on a 90-min ghost walk, starting from the Adam and Eve pub on Bishopsgate Tue and Thu at 1930 in Apr, May and Jun. Jul-Nov walks also run on a Mon. Walk only £6, under-16s £4; meal at the Adam and Eve pub and a walk £11.

Lowestoft, Great Yarmouth and around *p23*
Greyhound racing
Yarmouth Stadium, T01493-720343, www.yarmouthstadium.co.uk. Every Mon, Wed and Sat for greyhound racing throughout the year, races start at 1830 Mon and Wed and at 1930 on Sat.

Horse riding
Pakefield Riding School, Carlton Rd, Lowestoft, T01502-572257. 1-hr beach rides £28.

Swimming
Beccles Lido, Puddingmoor, T01502-713297, www.beccleslido.com. Open mid-May to mid-Sep. Next to the River Waveney is this traditional lido with a heated 30-m-long pool and toddler pool, surrounded by grass.

Theme parks
Pleasurewood Hills, Corton, Lowestoft, T01502-586000, pleasurewoodhills.com, £19, under-16s £16. Theme park with 40-m-high drop tower, rollercoaster, log flume and indoor laser game.

North coast from Cromer to King's Lynn *p30*
Boat trips
Bishop's Boats, Blakeney Quay, T01263-740753, T0800-074 0754 (freephone), www.bishopsboats.com. Seal-spotting 1-hr trips, £10, under-16s £5. Sometimes trips land on Blakeney Point, making the total trip last up to 2 hrs. Trips run at least once a day in spring and summer and up to 4 times daily in Aug. No trips Dec-Jan.
Coastal Voyager, Southwold, T07887-525082, www.coastalvoyager.co.uk. Offering a seal and wind farm trip, leaving from the harbour for Scroby Sands, off the coast of Great Yarmouth, where there are grey and common seals. £35, under-16s £18 for a 3-hr trip. Also 3½-hr trips up the River Blythe for £28, under-16s £18.
Temple's Seal Trips, T01263-740791, www.sealtrips.co.uk. Boats leave from Morston Quay for 1- or 2-hr trips to see the seals and land on Blakeney Point (NT), where there are tern colonies some months of the year and lots of other birdlife. Ticket office in **Anchor** pub, £9, under-16s £5.

⊖ Transport

Norwich *p19, map p20*
Air
Norwich airport (www.norwichairport.co.uk) has flights to **Aberdeen**, **Edinburgh**, **Exeter**, **Manchester** and **Newquay**, as well as other destinations in the Channel Islands and elsewhere in Europe.

Bus

By far the fastest, cheapest way to **London** by bus is with **Megabus**, T0900-1600 900 (61p a min), http://uk.megabus.com (3 hrs, £6). **National Express**, T08717-818178, www.nationalexpress.com, run direct services from Norwich Bus Station to **London Victoria** (from 4 hrs 45 mins) and every 2 hrs to **Stansted airport** (2 hrs 25 mins). They also have limited services to **Cambridge** (2 hrs 10 mins).

Train

Greater Anglia, T0845-600 7245, www.greateranglia.co.uk, runs the main service to and from Norwich. Trains are twice hourly to **London Liverpool Street** (1 hr 50 mins), every 20 mins to **Cambridge** (1 hr 10 mins) via Ely and twice hourly direct to **Ipswich** (40 mins). There is a regular service to **Stansted Airport** (1 hr 40 mins), changing at **Ely**.

Lowestoft, Great Yarmouth and around *p23*
Bus

National Express, T08705-808080, www.nationalexpress.com, run coaches to **London** to both Lowestoft (4 hrs 50 mins) and Great Yarmouth (4 hrs). First buses (www.firstgroup.com) have regular services to **Norwich** from Lowestoft (1 hr 15 mins) and Great Yarmouth (45 mins), continuing on to **Swaffham** and **King's Lynn**.

Train

From Great Yarmouth, trains run hourly to **Norwich**, 30 mins, with Greater Anglia (www.greateranglia.co.uk) and every 30 mins during peak periods. The Norwich trains pass through the Broads, including stations at **Reedham**, **Wroxham**, **Acle** and **Berney Arms**. Services to **London Liverpool Street** take 2 hrs 40 mins, via Norwich. From Lowestoft services to Norwich, 35 mins, run regularly. Trains to London Liverpool Street take 2 hrs 50 mins. As Great Yarmouth, trains to Norwich stop at stations in The Broads.

❶ Directory

Norwich *p19, map p20*
Hospitals Norfolk & Norwich University Hospitals, Colney La, Colney, T01603-286286, www.nnuh.nhs.uk.
Police Norfolk Constabulary, Bethel St, T01603-424242.

Contents

Footprint features

Suffolk

Suffolk is an odd county, famously known for being 'sleepy'. The arrival in recent years of large numbers of commuters fleeing London house prices has livened up the area considerably. And yet the good people of Suffolk cling fiercely to their rural roots, carefully preserving their wonderful old medieval wool towns and well-ordered little villages.

Bury St Edmunds is the capital of northwest Suffolk, a charming old place with a quietly prosperous air, a cathedral still in the process of completion, a beautiful Georgian theatre and fine central square dominated by the medieval abbey gatehouse. To the north, the almost deserted forests and heaths of Breckland stretch into Norfolk. To the south, one of the area's most popular tourist destinations is provided by the wool-enriched splendours of Lavenham, Long Melford and also Clare. To the southwest, Ipswich deserves a mention, not least for being the county's largest conurbation and its industrial powerhouse, squatting on the Orwell estuary and with a newly regenerated waterfront.

Which brings us to the coast, the county's pride and joy and an unmissable treat. From Woodbridge, high up the estuary of the river Deben, all the way to the dilapidated seaside entertainments at Lowestoft, the A12 runs just inland of some of England's most peculiar and memorable coastal towns, villages and scenery. Orford, with its Norman castle, smokehouses and eerie shingle Ness, is the first stop. Next up is Aldeburgh, famous for its classical music festival and increasingly for the émigré London novelists that stalk its long pebbly beach in the footsteps of composer Benjamin Britten. Then there is Southwold, which is even more classy, coupled with its arty little neighbour Walberswick.

Suffolk Coast from Ipswich to Southwold

Without doubt one of the most mysterious and enchanting stretches of coast in the south of England, declared an Area of Outstanding Natural Beauty, Suffolk's shoreline has also become distinctly fashionable. The character of the area is slowly changing as Londoners snap up holiday homes in their droves. And it's not hard to see why: the North Sea pounds along its pebbly beaches, seemingly intent on breaking inland to the ancient acres of forest at Rendlesham and Tunstall; at Orford Ness the waves have even moved tons of shingle down the coast forcing the river Alde to take a 10-mile detour south. Aldeburgh and Southwold are the seaside towns at the heart of the area, both still quite magical places to while away a few days. Between them lie the wildflower-strewn heaths of Dunwich and one of the RSPB's best reserves at Minsmere.

Visiting the Suffolk coast from Ipswich to Southwold

Getting there and around Greater Anglia Railways, T0845-600 7245, www.greater anglia.co.uk, runs the local **rail** service, with journeys direct from London Liverpool Street (one hour seven minutes) to Ipswich three times per hour. From Ipswich travel to Norwich (40 minutes) is twice hourly direct and to Cambridge direct (1 hour 20 minutes) is every hour. The local Greater Anglia stopping service runs every hour from Ipswich to Woodbridge, Wickham Market, Saxmunham, Halesworth, Beccles and Lowestoft (one hour 30 minutes). To Stansted Airport, change in Cambridge (two hours 20 minutes). **National Express**, T08717-818178, www.nationalexpress.com, runs a **bus** direct service from Ipswich to London Victoria (three hours 15 minutes) every two hours. Travel to Norwich (six hours 10 minutes) involves changing at Stansted Airport. Services to Cambridge via Stansted Airport (four hours) run every two hours. Buses to Stansted Airport take one hour 30 minutes and leave every two hours. Firstbuses, T0871-200 2233, www.firstgroup.com, serve most towns and villages in Suffolk and Norfolk.

Tourist information Aldeburgh TIC ① *48 High St, T01728-453637, atic@suffolk coastal.gov.uk, Easter-Sep daily 1000-1700, Oct-Easter Mon-Sat 1000-1500.* **Beccles** TIC ① *The Quay, Fen La, T01502-713196, May-Sep daily 0900-1300, 1400-1700.* **Felixstowe** TIC ① *91 Undercliff Rd West, T01394-276770, ftic@suffolkcoastal.gov.uk, Easter-Oct Mon-Sat 0900-1600, Sun 1000-1500.* **Ipswich** TIC ① *St Stephen's Church, St Stephen's La, T01473-258070, Mon-Sat 0900-1700.* **Lowestoft** TIC ① *East Point Pavilion, Royal Thoroughfare, T01502-533600, touristinfo@waveney.gov.uk, daily 1030-1700, opening at 1000 Sat-Sun.* **Southwold** TIC ① *69 High St, T01502-724729, southwold.tic@ waveney.gov.uk, Apr-Oct Mon-Fri 1000-1700, Sat 1000-1730, Sun 1100-1600, Nov-Mar Mon-Fri 1030-1530 (Wed closes at 1530), Sat 1000-1600.* **Woodbridge** TIC ① *Woodbridge Library, T01394-382240, Easter-Oct Mon-Fri 0900-1730, Sat 0930-1700, Sun 0930-1700, Oct-Easter Mon-Fri 0900-1730, Sat 1000-1700, Sun 1000-1300.*

Ipswich

The county town of Suffolk has suffered badly at the hands of the post-war developers, denying it much in the way of tourist trade and it has struggled to shrug off a reputation for being an ugly backwater. The waterfront docks have been attractively and significantly revamped and are now home to many bars and restaurants, as well as regular markets and other events. The town has a friendly and unpretentious atmosphere and some half-timbered buildings that survived the bombs in the Second World War give the city centre some charm.

A short walk from the centre, Christchurch Park contains the fine Tudor **Christchurch Mansion** ① *T01473 433554, Tue-Sun 1000-1700, free*, built on the site of an Augustinian Priory, once owned by Queen Elizabeth I's favourite Robert Devereaux, Earl of Essex. It holds the largest collection of Constable paintings outside London and also has works by Gainsborough and other Suffolk artists, along with a Tudor kitchen and Victorian toys. There's also a decent café.

On the High Street, the **Ancient House** is the best of the town centre old buildings, a pargeted and timbered Tudor confection, now a branch of Lakeland. Also on the High Street, **Ipswich Museum** ① *T01473-433551, Tue-Sat 1000-1700, free*, is a Suffolk natural history and wildlife museum with a woolly mammoth and a reconstructed Anglo-Saxon burial, although not quite as impressive as the real thing nearby at Sutton Hoo (see below).

The former **Cliff Brewery** was one of the oldest breweries in the country, run by Tolly Cobbold, until it closed in 2002, but its fine Victorian buildings still stand on the banks of the river Orwell and are under consideration for development. The **Brewery Tap** freehouse pub (www.brewerytap.org) is in the same location and serves some great local ales.

Woodbridge and around

Woodbridge itself is a small and attractive market town on the River Deben, as well as being something of a transport hub. The **Tide Mill** ① *T01394-385295, www.woodbridge tidemill.org.uk, May-Sep daily 1100-1700, Apr and Oct Sat-Sun 1100-1700, £3.50, under-16s £1.50*, its wheel dependent on the turning of the tides, dates from the 18th century. It was restored in the early 1970s and is now the last working tide mill in the country. On Market Hill, the **Woodbridge Museum** ① *5a Market Hill, T01394-380502, Easter-Oct Thu-Sun (daily during school holidays) and bank holidays 1000-1600, £1, under-16s 30p*, is a sweet local museum with an intriguing display on the local 19th-century translator and poet Edward Fitzgerald. A short distance out of town, on the B1079, **Buttrum's Mill** ① *T01473-264755, Apr-Sep Sun and bank holidays 1400-1730 (also Sat, May-Aug)*, was built in 1836, one of the finest tower windmills in the country and was used until 1928. Its huge sails are made up of almost 200 Venetian blind-style shutters, turned into the wind by the little six-bladed 'fantail'.

However, the best reason for a visit to Woodbridge is to see the extraordinary Anglo-Saxon burial site nearby at **Sutton Hoo** ① *3 miles east of Woodbridge on the B1083, T01394-389700, www.nationaltrust.org.uk, Apr-Oct daily 1030-1700, Jan-Mar and Nov-Dec Sat-Sun 1100-1600, £7.15, under-16s £3.70*. The National Trust visitor centre features a full-scale reconstruction of the famous Anglo-Saxon ship burial c AD 625 with original and replica artefacts, next door to the site of the discovery in 1939. There's a sincere attempt to illuminate the Dark Ages and a little room of finds, although the reconstruction of a grave is a bit spurious. The most significant finds are in the British Museum. Overlooking the mounds, Tranmere House was the Edwardian home of Edith Pretty, who instigated the archaeological excavations at Sutton Hoo. It is now restored to its 1930s glory. The site is set in 91 ha of woodland and is a good place for a walk.

In memoriam WG Sebald

On December 12, 2001, the German writer WG Sebald was killed in a car crash in Norwich at the age of 57. His death was an unspeakable loss to his family, friends and colleagues, while East Anglia also lost one of its most exceptional literary talents. With *The Rings of Saturn (Die Ringe des Saturn)* Sebald describes a partly fictional walk along the Suffolk coast from Lowestoft to Aldeburgh and beyond, that becomes a dreamlike evocation of the area's past, its associations, history and atmosphere. With intense precision, his prose details a morbid fascination with death and decay. The poignant irony of the fact that he too has joined the ranks of his favourite subject matter will never be lost on his still growing number of fans.

Aldeburgh and around

Aldeburgh itself is a tidy, tranquil little town stretched along the coast with only one main street. Not entirely successfully developed for tourism in the late 19th century, its fortunes later declined with its fishing fleet. The remnants of the fleet can be seen today, hauled up onto the shingle beach by winches, outside the picturesque fishermen's huts where you can buy freshly caught fish and shellfish. Things took a turn for the better thanks to classical music with the success of the **Aldeburgh Festival**, founded by Benjamin Britten in 1948 (now relocated to Snape Maltings nearby). Increasingly, houses in the town and on the seafront are being converted into holiday homes for the rich, and the town's prosperity has become more and more reliant on the tourist industry. The **marina** provides entertainment for yachty types but the place still has a genteel and faintly literary air.

Apart from strolling along the long Blue Flag pebbly beach (safe for swimming), enjoying top-notch fish and chips, or watching the sun rise out of the North Sea at dawn, there's not a whole lot to see or do in Aldeburgh itself, although it serves as an ideal base for explorations of the coast. The **Moot Hall** ① *www.aldeburghmuseumonline.co.uk, Apr-Oct daily 1430-1700, opening at 1200 Jun-Aug, 80p,* only a pebble's throw from the breakers, is a handsome timber-framed Tudor building that was once the town hall and stood in the middle of town. The town council still meets here today and the building is also now a museum. It contains some interesting old maps of the area in the council chamber, where Peter Grimes was tried in Britten's opera, and objects downstairs from the Snape Ship Burial, older by some years than Sutton Hoo, as well as other seafaring relics.

Take a short walk along the beach north of Aldeburgh towards Thorpeness (and the unmistakable landmark of Sizewell B nuclear power station) to see a giant scallop shell sculpture, *The Shell*, by Suffolk artist Maggi Hambling. The 4-m-high shell is dedicated to the composer Benjamin Britten, whose words 'I hear those voices that will not be drowned' from his opera *Peter Grimes* are inscribed on it.

Five miles inland from the town, **Snape Maltings** ① *T01728-688303, www.snapemaltings.co.uk,* is a concert hall standing on the beautiful reed-filled marshes and estuary on the River Alde. The main **Aldeburgh Music Festival** ① *T01728-453543, www.aldeburgh.co.uk,* is in June, but there are also the Proms in August, and an Early

Music festival usually in October, as well as regular concerts throughout the year. The interesting maltings buildings are also busy commercial enterprises, including house and garden shops, tea shop, café and a pub, as well as Hepworth sculptures and the Britton-Pears School of Music. There are some great walks around the marshes and estuary and river trips run from spring to autumn.

Orford and along the River Ore

Five miles south of Aldeburgh as the crow flies, although 12 by road, Orford is an attractive little red-brick Georgian town, nestling on the banks of the river Alde behind the strange shingle spit of Orford Ness and dominated by the 12th-century keep of **Orford Castle** ① *www.english-heritage.org.uk, T01394-450472, Apr-Sep daily 1000-1800, Oct daily 1000-1700, Nov-Mar Sat-Sun 1000-1600, £5.80, under-16s £3.50*. There are fabulous views over the marshes, river and town to the sea from the top of the castle. The town is home to a couple of smokeries, including the long-established family owned **Richardsons** ① *Baker's Lane, T01394-450103, www.richardsonssmokehouse.co.uk*, down a little alley off the High Street with piles of logs and smoke billowing out of a tar-covered wooden shack. They smoke just about everything edible, from garlic bulbs to gammon.

The town itself can become very crowded during summer, with Orford Quay a busy little boatyard. From here there are beautiful walks along the River Ore to the sound of tinkling halyards, a chance to spot wild geese, swans, and hares, although if you want to see the sea you'll have to cross to **Orford Ness National Nature Reserve** ① *www.nationaltrust.org.uk, T01394-450900, Apr-Oct 1000-1400 (Apr-Jun and Oct Sat only, Jul-Sep Tue-Sat), ferries from Orford Quay1000-1400, last return from the Ness at 1700, £8, children £4 including the ferry*, on the National Trust ferry. The largest vegetated shingle spit in Europe, it's littered with bizarre structures erected by the Ministry of Defence while it was a secret weapons research establishment from 1913 until the 1970s. Some buildings can be visited, including the former HQ, now housing a decommissioned atomic bomb. Given to the National Trust in 1993, the windswept desolation of the marshes, shingle and creek now provides a unique habitat for numerous rare flowers, mosses and lichens.

Another less happy story of the MOD's hand in the history of this coast is rumoured 7 miles further south down the coast, at the hamlet of **Shingle Street**, near the village of Hollesley and at the mouth of the River Ore. Here the coastguard's cottages are just about the only two-storey buildings in a line of individualistic bungalows lining another unique shingle strand opposite the end of Orford Ness and a Site of Special Scientific Interest. The eerie atmosphere of its pebbly beach is compounded by the existence of a secret file on the 'Evacuation of the population of Shingle Street' during the Second World War. Apparently underwater pipes full of petrol were tested here to repel invaders, setting the sea on fire and horribly burning the sappers, giving rise to gruesome tales of charred corpses being washed up on the beach. Nowadays, however, it's a popular spot for dog walking and night fishing.

North of Aldeburgh

Two miles north of Aldeburgh, **Thorpeness** is a holiday village purpose-built in the 1920s in an eccentric attempt to recreate the medieval atmosphere of 'merrie England' by a Scottish barrister. Nowadays that translates into a golf course, large boating lake and lots of

Walks on the Suffolk Coast

- **Orford**: 3 mile circle. Start: Orford harbour. A walk along the the River Alde overlooking Havergate Island and its birdlife, up the Ore and back to Orford. OS Maps: Explorer 212 Landranger 169/156.
- **Covehithe**: 2 miles there and back. Start: Covehithe village, 4 miles north of Southwold. A 10-minute walk along the low clifftop to the beach and then north along the beach to a lagoon and nature reserve. OS Maps: Explorer 231, Landranger 156.
- **Shingle Street**: 4 miles there and back. Start: Shingle Street. A walk along the eerie shingle beach landscape from the mouth of the Ore to Bawdsey (refreshments). OS Maps: Explorer 197, Landranger 169.
- **Tunstall Forest**: 2 mile circle. Start: 2 miles east of Tunstall on the B1078. A woodland walk through the ancient Forest of Aldewood, home to red squirrels, old conifers and oaks. OS Maps: Explorer 212, Landranger 156.
- **Dunwich Heath**: 3 mile circle. Start: Dunwich village. A walk up onto the wildflower National Trust heathland overlooking the sea. OS Map Explorer 231 Landranger 156.

half-timbered and clapperboard houses. The five-storey so-called House in the Clouds was an attempt to disguise the water tower by cladding it in wood and making it looks like a tall house, creating a somewhat bizarre landmark. Escape the crowds by walking along the attractive coastline, an unmistakable presence just north being the **Sizewell B** ① *T01728-653890, www.edfenergy.com, from late summer 2013 Mon-Fri 1000-1500*, nuclear power station which supplies enough electricity for the whole of Norfolk and Suffolk. Visits to the power station were suspended after 9/11 but the visitor centre will reopen in temporary premises in late summer 2013.

Four miles further north, **Minsmere** ① *T01728-648281, www.rspb.org.uk*, is one of the Royal Society for the Protection of Bird's best nature reserves, with wetland, woodland an coastal habitats. It's famous for its avocets, which can be seen in the spring (they head southwest in the summer) and other rare waders from hides overlooking the lagoons. There's a lovely walk down to the dyke near the **Eel Foot Inn** in Eastbridge (see below) and other waymarked trails. There are also also good activities for children, and a visitor centre, café and shop (daily 0900-1700, 1600 in winter).

A couple of miles further north is **Dunwich**, the Suffolk coast's famous lost town. In the Middle Ages it was one of the country's busiest seaports and boasted 14 churches, a 70-vessel fishing fleet and a population half as large as the City of London's. The story of its gradual collapse into the hungry sea is enthusiastically told at the **Dunwich Museum** ① *St James St, T01728-648796, www.dunwichmuseum.org.uk, Mar Sat-Sun 1400-1630, Apr-Sep daily, 1130-1630, Oct daily 1200-1600, free but donations welcome*. It includes a scale model of the town in its heyday as well as references to the many writers and artists – Henry James, Jerome K Jerome, Algernon Swinburne, WG Sebald and William Turner – who were inspired by its peculiar fate. All that can be seen today in the tiny village are the ruins of Greyfriars, a little wooden beach café – **Flora Tea Rooms**, which serves up fish and chips to rival those in Aldeburgh – and some crumbling cliffs. **Dunwich Heath** ① *T01728 648501, www.nationaltrust.org.uk*, a mile south of the village, is a wonderful purple and yellow heather-clad stretch of National Trust coastline, also with a tearoom and shop.

Inland from Aldeburgh

Twelve miles inland west of Aldeburgh, **Framlingham** is a delightful market town, much enhanced by **Framlingham Castle** ① *T01728-724189, www.english-heritage.org.uk, Apr-Sep daily 1000-1800, Oct daily 1000-1700, Nov-Mar Sat-Sun 1000-1600 (Feb half term open daily), £6.50, under-16s £3.90*, once the seat of the Dukes of Norfolk (the 3rd Duke was the uncle of Anne Boleyn and Catherine Howard), with remarkable and beautifully preserved tombs from the mid-16th century in the church of St Michael and superb views over the town from the remarkably complete 12th-century walls and their 13 towers, still looking much as they would have done when built. There's no central keep, but a 17th-century poor house survives inside, now home to an interesting display on moated buildings called the Lanman Museum.

Nine miles north of Framlingham, **Wingfield Old College** ① *Gardens and Galleries, Church Rd, Wingfield, www.wingfieldcollege.com*, is an unusual combination of an old school founded in 1362 alongside a handsome palladian mansion, with topiary gardens and a visual arts centre in the restored Great Barn.

Southwold and around

Twelve miles north up the coast from Aldeburgh, Southwold is an older, more sedate and picturesque seaside town, its Georgian townscape set back from the sea, perched up on the cliffs and grouped around several spacious greens laid out as firebreaks after a devastating conflagration in the 17th century. The home town of George Orwell, who despaired of its precious gentility, Southwold remains a very dignified resort. Down beside the beach and the row of brightly painted beach huts, the 190-m **pier** ① *T01502-722105, www.southwoldpier.co.uk*, was first constructed in 1900, but has undergone a series of renovation and rebuilding after storm damage. Its telescopes, tearoom and family amusements are just about the town's only concession to seaside tack.

Back in town, a charming 20-minute walk over the common and across the old iron footbridge brings you to **Walberswick**, even quieter and more rarified, the sort of place favoured by Sunday afternoon water colourists. This is a very popular spot for crabbing and also a small yacht haven. Its one pub, The Bell (www.bellinnwalberswick.co.uk), can become impossibly busy on sunny summer afternoons, although it also has a new addition, of the Barn Café, to cater for the crowds. In winter the little creekside village has a cosy and somnolent air.

Bury St Edmunds

Famous for its brewery, sugar beet and medieval abbey, Bury St Edmunds has the happy atmosphere of a town completely at ease with itself. It's easy to explore the compact centre of this attractive market town, with its medieval street plan still in evidence today, flanked by handsome Georgian buildings. 'Bury' to the locals, it's long been the pride of Suffolk, billing itself as the 'Shrine of a King, Cradle of the Law', reminders of the pilgrim's wealth that the medieval monastery accrued and the hospitality it offered to the barons forcing bad King John's hand to make a gesture towards democracy. Today Bury St Edmunds is the focus of the local farming community, pretty much slap bang in the middle of East Anglia.

Arriving in Bury St Edmunds

Getting there   The train station is on Station Hill, ¼ mile or a 15-minute walk north of the town centre via Northgate Street. There are also bus connections and a taxi rank outside. The bus station is less than five minutes' walk from the centre, on St Andrews Street North. ▸▸ *See Transport, page 64.*

Getting around   Bury St Edmunds is a small town with a partly pedestrianized centre; its layout is still based around the original medieval market town and is easy and pleasant enough to walk around. St Andrews St South/Cattle market is the main short stay car park four minutes' walk from main shopping centre.

Tourist information   Bury St Edmunds TIC ① *Angel Hill, T01284-764667, www.visit-bury stedmunds.co.uk, Easter-Oct Mon-Sat 0930-1700, May-Oct Sun 1000-1500, Nov-Easter Mon-Fri 1000-1600, Sat 1000-1300, bank holidays 1000-1500.* **Lavenham TIC** ① *Lady St, T01787-248207, http://www.southandheartofsuffolk.org.uk, mid-Mar-Oct daily 1000-1645, Nov-third week in Dec daily 1100-1500, Jan to mid-Mar Sat-Sun 1100-1500.* **Sudbury** TIC ① *Town Hall, Market Hill, T01787-881320, www.southandheartof suffolk.org.uk, Mon-Fri 0930-1600, Sat-Sun 1000-1530.*

Background

The town is named after the Anglo-Saxon king of East Anglia, who was martyred to the Danes in 869. After the Norman Conquest, Abbot Baldwin laid out a grid-iron street plan, the first of its kind in the country and still very much in evidence today. Less remains of one of the most powerful monasteries in medieval Europe, where the Barons forced King John to accept the need for Magna Carta, the famous 'bill of rights' that can be seen in Salisbury cathedral's chapter house.

Places in Bury St Edmunds

For visitors, the centre of Bury St Edmunds is **Angel Hill**, an attractive square overlooked by the imposing old abbey gatehouse. This great gateway was constructed in the early 14th century, and now leads into the fairly ordinary municipal gardens that were once the site of the old monastery. West of the gate, the compact size of Bury's town centre means that most of its sights can be seen in less than an hour's stroll around.

Abbeygate Street heads uphill a short distance to the **Buttermarket** and a trio of fine early 19th-century buildings. The neoclassical Corn Exchange stands at the top of Abbeygate, inscribed with the pious motto 'The Earth is the Lord's and the Fulness thereof'. Turning right, into Cornhill, another dignified square with a South African War Memorial in the middle, the third of the town centre's grand trio of buildings is now the contemporary art gallery **Smiths Row** ① *the Market Cross, T01284-762081, www.smithsrow.org, Tue-Sat 1030-1700, free,* housed in an elegant Georgian former theatre. The gallery stages interesting exhibitions and has a shop selling innovative craftworks and jewellery. On the opposite side of the square is the **Moyse's Hall** Museum ① *T01284-706183, www.moyseshall.org, Mon-Fri 1000-1700, Sat-Sun 1200-1600, £4, under-16s £2,* a local history museum featuring the Suffolk Regiment gallery in an 800-year-old building, possibly once a Jewish merchant's house.

Back at the top of Abbeygate Street, turning left instead of right, Guildhall Street heads south lined with attractive 17th-and 18th-century houses flanking the Guildhall itself with its 15th-century porch. Just beyond, another left turn leads back downhill along Churchgate Street, originally lined up with the Norman church's high altar. At the foot of the street stands the particularly fine Norman tower, all that remains of the church. Next to it is **St Edmundsbury Cathedral** ① *T01284-748720, www.stedscathedral.co.uk, daily 0830-1800, guided tours Apr-Sep Mon-Sat at 1130*, with its magnificent Gothic Millennium Tower completed after a five-year project starting in 2005 to look like Bell Harry at

Bury St Edmunds

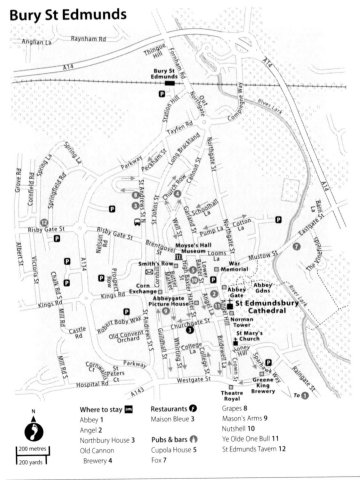

Where to stay 🛏	Restaurants 🍴	Grapes 8
Abbey 1	Maison Bleue 3	Mason's Arms 9
Angel 2		Nutshell 10
Northbury House 3	Pubs & bars 🍸	Ye Olde One Bull 11
Old Cannon	Cupola House 5	St Edmunds Tavern 12
Brewery 4	Fox 7	

Canterbury. Its nave was constructed in 1503, as part of the abbey of St Edmund, but ran out of funds. It was added to in the 1950s and again today. To one side there's a pleasant refectory with seats outside beside the old abbey walls, next to the Abbey Gardens, serving good-value homemade dishes such as steak and ale pie using locally sourced meat (open Monday-Saturday 0930-1530).

A right turn at the bottom of Churchgate Street leads into Crown Street, past **St Mary's Church** ① *T01284-754680, www.stmaryspeter.net/stmaryschurch, Mon-Fri 1000-1600 (winter 1500)*, which claims to be the third largest parish church in England. It has a spectacular nave and rare hammer-beam roof, as well as being the last resting place of 'Bloody' Mary Tudor.

Carrying straight on along Crown Street from St Mary's Church ends up at the **Greene King Brewery** ① *Westgate St, T01284-714297, www.greeneking.co.uk, museum and shop Mon-Fri 1030-1630, Sat 1030-1730, free, tours (1 hr 45 mins, £9) of the brewery Mon-Sat at 1400, Wed-Sat also at 1100, Sat also at 1230, 1530, Sun at 1130, Apr-Sep also on Thu at 1900, £11*, where beer has been brewed continuously since 1799 and where the company runs a small and accomplished promotion of its product. There are great views of the town from the roof of the brewery's art deco Brewhouse. The **Brewery Tap** pub provides the freshest possible Old Speckled Hen, Abbot Ale and Ruddles County.

Beyond the Brewery, at the end of Westgate, the thriving **Theatre Royal** ① *T01284-769505, www. theatreroyal.org, open door visits on Tue and Thu 1400-1600 and on Wed and Sat 1030-1300, £3.50, guided tours lasting 1 hr 20 mins on Tue and Thu at 1400 and Sat and Wed at 1100, £6, open door and guided tours free to National Trust members, all times subject to change due to rehearsals and performances*, is the only existing Regency theatre in the country. Built in 1819, it underwent a major £5 million project in 2007 to restore many Georgian architectural features. It is now owned by Greene King and the National Trust, and still stages some good quality touring productions.

Around Bury St Edmunds

Three miles southwest of Bury St Edmunds on the A143, at Horringer, the National Trust **Ickworth House** ① *T01284-735270, www.nationaltrust.org.uk, parkland and woods daily 0800-2000, Rotunda mid-Mar to Nov Mon-Tue and Fri-Sun 1100-1700, Mar-Oct also Thu 1200-1500, Nov to mid-Dec Sat-Sun 1100-1600, Italianate Gardens daily 1000-1600, until 1730 mid-Mar to Nov, £12, under-16s £6, gardens only £3.10 (winter), £5 (summer), under-16s free or £2.20*, was long the seat of the Hervey family, eccentric Earls of Bristol since the early 18th century, who transformed the place at the end of that century into a palatial neoclassical showpiece complete with unusual lozenge-shaped domed Rotunda gallery. The basement of the Rotunda has recently been restored to show life below the stairs in 1910. Highlights of the interior are the library, with its 18th-century furniture, and the collection of Gainsboroughs, a Titian and a Velasquez. The 728 ha park provides delightful walks with views of this grandiose monument to an ecclesiastical grandee with ideas way above his station. It now also has the luxury Ickworth Hotel in the East Wing, as well as four holiday cottages.

Seven miles northwest of Bury St Edmunds on the A1101, at West Stow, an **Anglo-Saxon Village** ① *Icklingham Rd, T01284 728718, www.weststow.org, daily 1000-1700, £6, under-16s £4, guided tours 1130 and 1430*, has been reconstructed on the actual site, unusually enough, of a seventh-century settlement. Deserted, unless on fancy dress days, surrounded by firs and gorse in the 15 ha West Stow Country Park, with an adventure playground, and the lowland heath of the Brecks, it still just about manages to evoke an atmosphere. In the visitor centre, there are finds from the site and explanations of the local archaeology.

Five miles east of Bury, are the medieval murals in **St Ethelbert's Church**, Hesset, near the Woolpit junction south off the A14 between Bury and Stowmarket. Particularly well preserved is a mural from 1460 of the Seven Deadly Sins in the north aisle, each standing in a dragon's mouth, Sloth too idle to clamber out, the others all suspended beneath the over-arching figure of Pride.

Lavenham, Long Melford and Clare

Ten miles southeast of Bury via the A134 and A1141 is Lavenham, the most visited and picturesque old inland town of Suffolk and famous for its many well-preserved medieval timber-framed buildings. Along with Long Melford and Clare, a short distance west in the Stour valley, these three small towns still most perfectly express the wool-rich elegance of the 16th and 17th centuries. Lavenham is the most tourist-orientated, even going so far as to boast an audio tour of the town available from the local pharmacy as punters wonder at the galleries of local contemporay art and many independent shops, including a number selling antiques and knitwear. knitwear shops and antiques shops. The old Swan Hotel, the Crooked House Gallery, and Greyhound pub are strung along the main street, the A1141, along with an impressive array of half-timbered, plastered and pargeted houses. But the **Market Place** on top of the hill is the real highlight of the town, along with its mini-cathedral of a church, a 20-minute walk south. The **Guildhall** ① *T01787-247646, www.nationaltrust.org.uk/lavenham-guildhall, Mar-Nov daily 1100-1700, Nov-Dec Sat-Sun 1100-1600, £4.45, under-16s £1.80*, is a 16th-century timber-framed building on the Market Place with a small local history museum, walled garden and displays on the wool trade, including a working loom, and agriculture. Also in the Market Place is the **Little Hall**, a medieval hall house and nearby in Water Street, the Priory, converted into a home by a wealthy merchant at around the same time.

Lavenham church was built in the 15th century to rival Long Melford's, by the De Veres of Hedingham Castle and the clothiers called Spring. Restrained and serene, the length of the nave, the height of the tower and beautiful chancel arch make it an extraordinary parish church.

Four miles west of Lavenham, nestling in the valley of the river Stour, **Long Melford** lives up to its name as it stretches along its single main street just above the river, a mecca for antique dealers. The medieval church of the Holy Trinity here is reckoned by many to be the most splendid in Suffolk. The outside of the tower was redone in the early 20th century but inside there's a magnificent procession of stained glass, including a window supposed to have inspired John Tenniel's illustrations for *Alice in Wonderland* and a rare Lily Crucifix.

Nearby, across the green, similar in date to the Tudor almshouses that cluster around the church, **Melford Hall** ① *T01787-376395, www.nationaltrust.org.uk, Apr-Oct Wed-Sun and bank holiday Mon 1300-1700, £6.60, under-16s £3.20*, has been lived in by the Hyde Parkers since the late 18th century, a fine red brick house where Elizabeth I was once entertained in lavish style by Sir William Cordell. Now two magnificent copper beeches set off its front lawns, with an adorable octagonal Elizabethan gazebo set into its wisteria-covered garden wall. Inside there's an impressive library and staircase, and unusual pictures done by Beatrix Potter, once a regular visitor to the house.

Six miles west of Long Melford, **Clare** is another old wool-rich town in the Stour valley, smaller and less touristy than Melford or Lavenham, set in good walking country with an attractive old high street and sweet country park surrounding the grassy remains of the town's **Norman castle**. The church of **St Peter and St Paul** is another perpendicular masterpiece, flooded with light and medieval faces looking down from the ceiling which avoided the iconoclast Dowsing's attempt to shoot them down.

Pakenham Water Mill ① *T07585-899633, pakenhamwatermill.org.uk, Apr-Sep Thu 1000-1600, Sat-Sun and Bank Holidays 1330-1700 (Jul-Aug open from 1200), milling demonstrations on Thu at 1000-1100, £3.50, under-16s £2*, is a working windmill and watermill run by the Suffolk Preservation Society. The 18th-century watermill is the last of its kind in operation in Suffolk. Home-ground flour is also available.

Suffolk listings

Where to stay

For hotel and restaurant price codes and other relevant information, see pages 9-12.

Suffolk coast from Ipswich to Southwold *p49*

££££ Crown Hotel, 90 High St, Southwold, T01502-722275, adnams.co.uk. The slightly less formal Adnams award-winning option with an excellent restaurant and bar. Rates include breakfast and dinner.

££££ Hintlesham Hall, Hintlesham, 4 miles west of Ipswich, T01473-652334, www.hintleshamhall.co.uk. Easily the best top-end option in the area, a grand Elizabethan country house with charming beamed rooms in an annexe and a restaurant with a good reputation. There is also a spa, gym and pool.

££££-£££ Bell Inn, Ferry Rd, Walberswick, T01502-723109, www.bellinn walberswick.co.uk. Cosy old pub with estuary and harbour views.

££££-£££ Crown and Castle, Orford, T01394-450205 www.crownand castlehotel.co.uk. The top place to stay in Orford, a renovated restaurant with stylish rooms and a decent restaurant, **Trinity**.

£££ Eel's Foot Inn, Eastbridge, T01728-830154, www.theeelsfootinn.co.uk. A great B&B about 400 m from RSPB Minsmere and less than an hour's walk to the coast along a footpath. Rooms overlook the marsh, Cycle hire. See also Pubs, page 62.

£££ King's Head, Front St, Orford, T01394-450271, www.thekingshead orford.co.uk. A good B&B option in a pub offering rooms with flatscreen TVs and bathrobes. Good food served in the bar.

£££ Melton Hall, Melton, near Woodbridge, T01394-388138, meltonhall.co.uk. Lovely B&B in a Georgian house in its own fine grounds.

£££ Old Rectory, Campsea Ashe, Woodbridge, T01728-746524, www.theoldrectorysuffolk.com. A stylish Georgian rectory set in over 1 ha of gardens with an excellent restaurant.

£££ Salthouse Harbour Hotel, Neptune Quay, Ipswich, T01473-226789, www.salthouse harbour.co.uk. Sister to the **Angel Hotel** in Bury St Edmunds, this designer hotel in a former Victorian warehouse on the quay has fantastic views over the marina, exposed brick walls, plenty of modern art and custom-made contemporary furniture. Rooms have flatscreen TVs, great toiletries and Wi-Fi; some also have a balcony overlooking the water and freestanding baths, There's a good restaurant with an comprehensive wine list.

£££ The Ship at Dunwich,
St James St, Dunwich, T01728-648219, www.shipatdunwich.co.uk. This pub has comfortable, snug little rooms, some of which overlook the sea and the marsh.

£££ Westleton Crown, The Street, Westleton, near Southwold, T01728-648777, www.westletoncrown.co.uk. Run by the same company as **The Ship at Dunwich**, this refurbished coaching inn has stylish rooms offering goose down duvets, flatscreen TVs and Egyptian cotton linen. There's an award-winning restaurant and Suffolk ales are on tap in the bar. The hotel's claim to fame is that the Duke and Duchess of Cambridge stayed here in 2012. Recommended.

£££-££ Swan Hotel, Market Pl, Southwold, T01502-722186, adnams.co.uk. The local brewers Adnams pretty much have the local hotel accommodation sewn up, and this is their flagship. Great for a traditional tea.

££ Jolly Sailor, Quay St, Orford, T01394-450243, jollysailororford.co.uk. Cheap and cheerful B&B offering 2-night minimum stays only.

Aldeburgh and around *p51*

£££ The Brudenell, The Parade, Aldeburgh, T01728-452071, www.brudenellhotel.co.uk. One of the town's best hotels is on the southern tip of the town, with a fine terrace for cocktails overlooking the sea and modern, comfortable rooms.

£££ Ocean House, 25 Crag Path, Aldeburgh, T01728-452094, www.oceanhouse aldeburgh.co.uk. Good B&B option right on the beach with pleasant family atmosphere. Deservedly immensely popular, so booking well ahead essential, preferably for the sea view room on the first floor.

£££ Wentworth Hotel, at the northern end of the prom in Aldeburgh, T01728-452312, www.wentworth-aldeburgh.com. This place

has been top of the range for traditional teas and sea view chintzy rooms since 1920.

£££ White Lion Hotel, Market Cross Pl, Seafront, Aldeburgh, T01728-452720, www.whitelion.co.uk. Not quite as grand as the **Wentworth Hotel**, but has a pleasant oak-panelled restaurant and contemporary, comfortable rooms, some overlooking the Moot Hall and the beach, at a price. Free Wi-Fi and some Sky channels.

Self-catering

£££ Martello Tower, right at the southern tip of Aldeburgh, book well in advance via the Landmark Trust, T01628-825925, www.landmarktrust.org.uk. A round Napoleonic fort guarding the approach to Orford Ness with 2 twin rooms.

££ Crabbe Cottage, Crabbe St, Aldeburgh T07967-339424, www.crabbecottage.co.uk. Cosy self-catering house in a quiet street close to the beach. No children or pets allowed.

Bury St Edmunds *p54, map p56*

£££ Abbey Hotel, 35 Southgate St, T01284-762020, www.abbeyhotel.co.uk. Reasonable option in handsome Tudor and medieval buildings retaining many original features. There's spacious accommodation in outbuildings although fairly cramped rooms upstairs, and welcoming staff. Free Wi-Fi.

£££ The Angel Hotel, Angel Hill, T01284-753926, www.theangel.co.uk. Old ivy-clad coaching inn opposite the Abbey gate, done up in a contemporary way, with vintage furniture and chic decor. The most central address in Bury, it's famous as the location where Dickens wrote some of *The Pickwick Papers*. Friendly and very helpful staff. Wi-Fi and breakfast included. Sister hotel to the **Salthouse Harbour** in Ipswich (see below).

£££ Old Cannon Brewery, Cannon St, T01284-768769, www.oldcannon brewery.co.uk. B&B with comfortable rooms located in a modern micro-brewery and freehouse in an old Victorian building a short walk to the east of the centre, with a restaurant.

£££-££ Northbury House, 7 Northgate St, T01284-754617, www.northburyhouse.co.uk. Smart B&B in a historic building a near the centre with well-equipped rooms. Good breakfast included.

Around Bury St Edmunds *p57*

££££ Swan Hotel, Lavenham, T01787-247477, www.theswanat lavenham.co.uk. The most upmarket option in town, with lots of exposed beams and panelling. Smart rooms with flatscreen TVs and free Wi-Fi. There are mementoes of Second World War airmen in the bar.

££££-£££ Great House Restaurant and Hotel, Lavenham, T01787-247431, www.greathouse.co.uk. Award-winning restaurant (see page 62) and hotel in an elegant Georgian house with muted decor in French grey and green. The 5 stylish rooms are equipped with Wi-Fi, mini-bar, espresso machines and Egyptian linen. Attentive and efficient French staff.

£££ Angel Hotel, Market Pl, Lavenham, T01787-247388, www.wheelersangel.com. Recently renovated by Marco Pierre White as part of his Wheeler's of St James's chain, this historic Tudor inn has bags of character, including lots of exposed beams and sloping floors, and a superb restaurant. However, some of the rooms are in need of refurbishment.

££ Brighthouse Farm, Melford Rd, Lawshall, T01284-830385, www.brighthouse farm.co.uk. Roberta Truin offers a warm welcome at her 18th-century farmhouse B&B with 1-ha garden. There is also self-catering accommodation and a campsite.

££ Church Farm, Bradfield Combust, T01284-386333, www.church farm-bandb.co.uk. Good value B&B in an 18th-century house on a working fruit farm.

Suffolk coast from Ipswich to Southwold *p49*

££ The Anchor Inn, Walberswick, T01502-722112, www.anchorat walberswick.com. Uses fresh local ingredients for dishes served at lunch and dinner. Barbecues in the summer and curries on Fri evenings. Also offers rooms, some with sea views.

££ Butley Orford Oysterage, Market Hill, Orford, T01394-450277, www.pinneysof orford.co.uk. Open daily. Serves fantastic very fresh seafood including their own farmed oysters in simple surroundings; excellent value and often very busy. Also has a shop on the quay selling products from their smokery and fresh fish caught by them.

££ The Captain's Table, 3 Quay St, Woodbridge, T01394-383145, captains table.co.uk. Closed Sun and Mon. A pleasant little local seafood restaurant serving good-value dishes, with tables outside.

££ King's Head, Gorman's La, Laxfield, T01986-798395, www.laxfieldkings head.co.uk. Thatched pub with plenty of original features, including a tap room, settles and an ancient fireplace. It does very good real ales and a hearty homemade menu for lunch and supper. (Laxfield was the birthplace of iconoclast William Dowsing.)

££ Mariners, Neptune Quay, Ipswich, T01473-289748, www.marinersipswich.co.uk. Run by the same people as **The Great House** in Lavenham and **Maison Bleue** in Bury St Edmunds, this French brasserie offers an excellent menu at very reasonable prices. The restaurant is located on a restored Victorian boat moored on a quay.

£ The Coastguards Tearooms, Dunwich Heath, T01728-648505. A National Trust tearoom with views of the sea and fresh homemade cakes.

£ The Lord Nelson, East St, Southwold, T01502-722079, www.thelordnelson

southwold.co.uk. A cosy pub close to the cliff-top seafront, with fresh traditional food.

£ Parish Lantern, Village Green, Walberswick, T01502-723173. A tea room in a listed building with a beautiful garden in the middle of the village.

£ White Horse in Rendham, T01728-663497, www.whitehorserendham.co.uk. Come here for traditional bar food, local real ales and open fires.

Aldeburgh and around *p51*
Aldeburgh is well supplied with good restaurants along its High St, thanks in part to the fastidious tastes of weekending Londoners.

£££-££ 152, 152 High St, Aldeburgh, T01728-454594, 152aldeburgh.com. Good-value dishes served up in a mellow environment that's been around some time.

££ The Lighthouse, 77 High St, Aldeburgh, T01728-453377, www.lighthouse restaurant.co.uk. An old-timer, a breezy café during the day, serving an accomplished modern menu in the evenings. Booking advisable.

££ Regatta, 171 High St, Aldeburgh, T01728-452011, www.regattaaldeburgh.com. A restaurant with a seafaring theme specializing locally caught tasty fish seafood.

£ Aldeburgh Fish and Chip Shop, High St, Aldeburgh, T01728-454685, www.aldeburghfishandchips.co.uk. Considered by many to be the best fish and chip shop in the country. It's very popular so be prepared to queue, but it's worth the wait. Also owns the **Golden Galleon** just along the High St. Recommended.

Bury St Edmunds *p54, map p56*
£££-££ Maison Bleue, 30 Churchgate St, T01284-760623, www.maisonbleue.co.uk. Closed Mon and Sun. Very well-prepared French fish dishes in a stylish setting, easily one of the best restaurants in town.

Around Bury St Edmunds *p57*
££ The Great House, see page 61. Award-winning restaurant serving excellent French food in an attractive old house with dining outside in the inner courtyard.

££ The Star Inn, Lidgate, T01638-500275, www.lidgatestar.co.uk. This award-winning pub-cum-restaurant in an attractive 16th-century building uses locally sourced ingredients for dishes on its Mediterranean-influenced menu. There are also good tapas options.

£ The Beehive, Horringer, near Ickworth, T01284-753260, beehivehorringer.net. This pretty flintstone pub on the fringe of Ickworth park has a good menu of Thai dishes.

🔊 Pubs, bars and clubs

Suffolk coast from Ipswich to Southwold *p49*
Butt and Oyster, Pin Mill, near Chelmondiston on the B1456 from Ipswich, T01473-780764, www.debeninns.co.uk. A very popular and famous riverside pub with excellent rustic-style dishes, Unfortunately it's often almost too busy for its own good in the summer.

The Eel's Foot Inn, see Where to stay, page 59. This pub and B&B does decent enough pub grub with locally sourced ingredients. There is also a quiet, pretty garden overlooking Minsmere bird reserve. Regular live music, with folk every Thu and occasional events at weekends.

Fat Cat Pub, 288 Spring Rd, Ipswich, T01473-726524, www.fatcatipswich.co.uk. Does some top real ales and has a good little beer garden.

The Victoria, on the A1120 in Earl Soham, T01728-685758. A country pub worth checking out. An outlet for the tiny Earl Soham Brewery near the pub in the village.

Aldeburgh and around *p51*
Ship, Blaxhall, 6 miles from Aldeburgh, T01728-688316, www.blaxhallshipinn.co.uk.

Good pub for locally brewed real ales and home-cooked food, specializing in seafood from the local area. It's also a B&B.

White Hart, 222 High St, Aldeburgh, T01728-453205. Especially popular with the locals.

Ye Olde Crosse Keys,
Crabbe St, T01728-452637, www.aldeburgh-crosskeys.co.uk. Right on the seafront with tables outside, the best pub for genial conversations with strangers.

Bury St Edmunds *p54, map p56*
Nutshell, The Traverse, top of Abbeygate St, T01284-764867, www.thenutshellpub.co.uk. This place stands out for being the smallest pub in England, with a bar that can only accommodate about 8 people.

Other pubs worth seeking out for the quality of their ales and/or pleasant atmosphere include the **Mason's Arms**, Whiting St, www.masonspub.co.uk; **St Edmunds Tavern**, Risbygate St; **The Fox**, Eastgate St, www.thefoxinnbury.co.uk; **The Grapes**, St Andrews St North, well-known for its live music, and **Ye Olde One Bull**, Angel Hill in the middle of town, which brews its own beer.

⊙ Entertainment

Ipswich *p49*
Art galleries
Ipswich Art School Gallery, High St, T01473-433681. Tue-Sun 1000-1700, free. The town's former art school – whose former students Maggi Hambling, the artist who created *The Shell* sculpture in Aldeburgh (see page 51) and musician Brian Eno – has reopened as an art gallery showing contemporary art.

Cinema
Ipswich Film Theatre, Corn Exchange, Kings Street, T01473-433100, www.iftt.co.uk. Screens independent and world cinema films.

Theatre
DanceEast, Jerwood DanceHouse, T01473-295230, www.danceeast.co.uk. In a new custom-built venue on the waterfront, Danceeast stages regular and varied dance shows.

New Wolsey Theatre, Civic Dr, T01473-295900, www.wolseytheatre.co.uk. Own theatre productions and performances by touring companies.

Regent Theatre & Corn Exchange, 3 St Helens St, T01473-433100, www.ipswichregent.com. East Anglia's largest theatre and also a concert venue.

Bury St Edmunds *p54, map p56*
Art galleries
Smiths Row, see page 55.

Cinema
Abbeygate Picture House, 4 Hatter St, T0871-902 5722, www.picturehouses.co.uk. One of the county's oldest cinemas, dating back to the 1920s, has been newly refurbished and screens classic films as well as the latest releases, Small café-bar serving great snacks, beer and wine which you can take in to enjoy whilst you watch a film. Usherettes and sofas for couples complete the intimate, retro atmosphere.

Theatre
Theatre Royal, see page 57.

⊙ Festivals

Jun Aldeburgh Festival,
www.aldeburgh.co.uk. Annual famous classical music festival, celebrating the centenary of Benjamin Britten's birth in 2013.
Jun Ipswich Arts Festival, www.ip-art.com. Month-long arts festival, also known as **Ip Art**, with loads of events featuring a free annual music event held in Christchurch Park; past headlining acts have included Ed Sheeran.

⚑ What to do

Aldeburgh and around *p51*
Aldeburgh Yacht Club, Slaughden Rd,
Aldeburgh, T01728-452562,
www.aldeburghyc.org.uk. Sailing events at
weekends throughout the summer.
Lady Florence, T07831-698298,
www.lady-florence.co.uk. A converted 50ft
Admiralty supply vessel, leaves from Orford
Quay, for 3-course American brunch cruises,
watching the birdlife, up and down beside
Orford Ness. Brunch cruises of just over 2 hrs
or 3½-hr lunch or dinner cruises start at
around £20.

⊖ Transport

**Suffolk coast from Ipswich to
Southwold** *p49*
Bicycle hire
Alton Cycle Hire, Alton Reservoir, Holbrook
Rd, Stutton, Ipswich, T01473-328873,
www.altoncyclehire.co.uk.
Byways Bicycles, Priory La, Darsham, near
Saxmundham, T01728-668764, www.byways
bicycles.co.uk. Bikes for hire by day or week.

Car
Fleetway Car and Van Hire, 110 Bramford
Rd, Ipswich, T01473-231888. **National**, 538
Woodbridge Rd, Ipswich, T01473-724665,
www.nationalcar.co.uk. **Thrifty**, 549a
Wherstead Rd, Ipswich, T01473-240822,
www.thrifty.co.uk.

Taxi
B Dobson, 29 Linden Cl, Aldeburgh,
T01728-454116. **M&R Cars**, Woodbridge
Railway Station, T01394-386661,
www.mandrcars.co.uk. **Southwold Private
Hire**, T01502-726040,
www.southwoldprivatehire.co.uk.

Train
There are regular services to **London
Liverpool Street** from Ipswich (1 hr 10 mins)
or Ely (1 hr). There are also services daily to
Bury St Edmunds from Ipswich (30 mins)
and to **Cambridge** (1 hr 20 mins) operated
by **Greater Anglia** (www.greateranglia.co.uk).

Bury St Edmunds *p54, map p56*
Bury St Edmunds is about 80 miles from
London by **road** (1½ hours). Take the M11
North and at junction 9 take the A11 then the
A14 to Bury St Edmunds.

Bus
National Express, T08705-808080, run
services (3 hrs 25 mins) to **London Victoria**
from Bury St Edmunds bus and coach station,
via Cambridge (30 mins' stop). There are
limited direct services (2 hrs 10 mins).

Car
Europcar, Dettingen Way, T01284-355502,
www.europcar.co.uk; **Enterprise**, Prospect
Row, T01284-748784, www.enterprise.co.uk;
Thrifty, Station Hill, T01284-702 195,
www.thrifty.co.uk.

Taxi
The main taxi rank in Bury St Edmunds is on
Cornhill, and there is another at the Railway
Station. Local minicab firms include: **A1 Cars
Cars**, T01284-766777, www.a1cars.co.uk; **ABA
Taxis**, T01284-767829a;, T01284-762288 and
Tudor Cars, T01284-754245.

Train
To **London Liverpool Street** from Bury St
Edmunds via Ipswich (1 hr 55 mins) or to
London Kings Cross via Cambridge or Ely
(1 hr 40 mins). There are regular train services
daily between Bury St Edmunds and **Ipswich**
(35 mins) and **Cambridge** (40 mins)
operated by **Greater Anglia**
(www.greateranglia.co.uk).

Contents

Footprint features

Cambridgeshire

Apart from the university town at its heart, Cambridgeshire is not a particularly prepossessing place to visit. Its fertile soil and the demands of agribusiness have created a dull and lifeless landscape across large areas, although the few areas of high or wooded ground are consequently all the more interesting.

Cambridge itself draws in millions of visitors each year to admire its colleges' world-class museums and string of well-run festivals. A relatively small and undeniably very pretty town, it's mobbed most of the year with students and tourists who give it a lively buzz on the streets. In summer, a punt along the river here is still a must for a full appreciation of the place. The river winds out to Grantchester, the village immortalized by the poet Rupert Brooke, but only one of a series of endearing Cambridge satellite settlements such as Trumpington.

To the south of the city, off the M11, is the Imperial War Museum's vast museum of militarized flight at Duxford, just before the unexpected prominence of the mystical Gog Magog Hills. To the north, Ely Cathedral sails majestically above the well-drained farmland all around, the Queen of the Fens.

Cambridge and around

More than anything else, Cambridge is its university. Unlike Oxford, its traditional rival, the city would otherwise be little more than a fairly unremarkable market town south of the Wash. For the last 700 years or so, academia has made its mark in this little place more impressively than just about anywhere else in the world. If it's old colleges you want to see, with their medieval and Renaissance chapels, libraries, halls, gardens and courts, Cambridge is the place to come. Partly because of the tourist pressure, the whole town has a slightly unreal, self-conscious atmosphere, an impression compounded by the type of twee flannels-and-blazers pastoral idyll once promoted by the cult surrounding local poet Rupert Brooke. Women were admitted to the University in 1947 though, the first in a series of reforms that has turned it into one of the most dynamic centres for research in the country, building on its strengths in mathematics and the sciences.

The city itself, only granted that status in the 1950s, now has a growing population of about 120,000, drawn in to work for the high-tech industries discreetly placed along the ring road. ▶ *For listings, see pages 77-82.*

Arriving in Cambridge

Getting there Cambridge **train** station is on Station Road, a 20-minute walk from the centre. There are frequent direct trains from London. From London take M11 north (which passes close to Stansted airport and Saffron Walden), at Junction 13 take the A1303 east and follow signs to city centre (1 hour 15 minutes, 63 miles from central London). Cambridge is well served by express **coach** services, all of which terminate at the Drummer Street coach stands, adjacent to the bus station in the centre of the city. ▶ *See Transport, page 81.*

Getting around Cambridge town centre is only about a mile or so in diameter bordered to the north and west by the river Cam and the river Granta and its green banks which include the Midsummer Common and Jesus Green. The town centre is easily navigated by foot or by bicycle. The main shopping centre is largely pedestrianized and there are many cycle lanes on the main roads and through the many parks in the city centre.

Tourist information Cambridge TIC ⓘ *Guildhall, Peas Hill, T0871-226 8006, www.visitcambridge.org, Mon-Sat 1000-1700, Apr-Oct Sun and bank holidays 1100-1500,* has helpful staff.

Background

As its name suggests, Cambridge owes its existence to its location at a solid bridgeable point on the river Cam. A settlement called Camboritum grew up here, at the junction of Akeman Street (between London and King's Lynn) and the Via Devana (between Lincoln and Colchester). The Romans established a fort on the outer bend of the river, on the spot later chosen by the Normans for their castle, just over Magdalene Bridge (Castle Mound marks the place today). Medieval myth-making aside (one legend has it that the University was founded by none other than King Arthur), the received wisdom is that the University as such first took shape thanks to scholars fleeing riots in Oxford in 1209. They soon made themselves unpopular with the locals, resulting in the burning of the

Cambridge

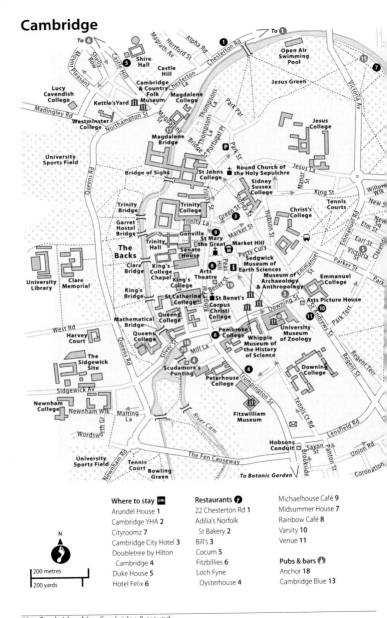

Where to stay 🛏
Arundel House 1
Cambridge YHA 2
Cityroomz 7
Cambridge City Hotel 3
Doubletree by Hilton
  Cambridge 4
Duke House 5
Hotel Felix 6

Restaurants 🍴
22 Chesterton Rd 1
Adilia's Norfolk
  St Bakery 2
Bill's 3
Cocum 5
Fitzbillies 6
Loch Fyne
  Oysterhouse 4

Michaelhouse Café 9
Midsummer House 7
Rainbow Café 8
Varsity 10
Venue 11

Pubs & bars 🍸
Anchor 18
Cambridge Blue 13

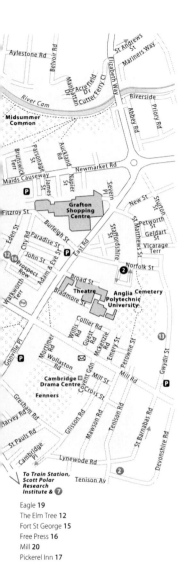

University records in St Mary's church and the subsequent execution of 18 townsmen. Church and Royalty favoured the scholars and they prospered. The first major phase of the University's expansion occurred after the Black Death in 1349, when, as in the country as a whole, almost half the town's population was wiped out. Colleges sprang up along the course of the old High Street, now King's Parade and Trinity Street, while the University's European status and reputation was confirmed with the arrival of Erasmus in the early 16th century. Despite dissolving the monasteries, Henry VIII chose to demonstrate his munificence with the foundation of Trinity but stole much of the other colleges' silver. As a result, they were forced to open their doors to the rich and compromise their scholastic ideals. In the 17th century, Cambridge was at the centre of the Puritan revival, shaping the ideology that inspired the Civil War and also exporting it to the colonies of America. Oliver Cromwell briefly attended Sidney Sussex as a commoner. Surprisingly perhaps, after the Restoration and then the Glorious Revolution of 1688, the University became staunchly Royalist and Tory: like Oxford, during the 18th century it earned a reputation for debauching the sons of the gentry. Victorian Cambridge saw the salvation of the University's credibility with stunning developments in science, nurturing greats like Charles Darwin, electrical pioneer James Clerk-Maxwell, and in the early 20th century electron-discover JJ Thompson and atom-splitter Ernest Rutherford. Philosophy too was a strong subject, thanks to Ludwig Wittgenstein and Bertrand Russell. During the 1930s the University bred an alarming number of Stalinist sympathizers, culminating in the celebrated traitors Burgess, Blunt, Philby and Maclean.

Orientation

Market Hill, a square where a general market still takes place Monday to Saturday, is the centre of Cambridge, with the Guildhall and TIC on its south side. Most of the colleges of particular interest to a visitor are lined up along Trinity Street a few steps to the west down St Mary's Street past the church of St Mary the Great. The University church and parish church of Cambridge is not that spectacular but has a fine oak roof donated by Henry VII, reconstructed at the end of the 15th century. St Mary's Street brings you out on Trinity Street opposite Senate House, the University's headquarters, and the Old Schools behind. Turning right here heads north. Turning left, south.

South of Market Hill

Top of most visitors' places to visit is **King's College** ⓘ *King's Parade, T01223-331100, www.kings.cam.ac.uk, during term-time: Mon-Sat 0930-1530, choral evensong 1730, Sun 1315-1415, choral evensong 1030, 1530, vacations daily 0930-1630 (no services), the chapel is occasionally closed for recordings and concerts, £7.50, 12-15 year olds £5, under-12s free*, for the spectacular chapel on the north side of its Great Court, with the world's largest fan vault and some impressive medieval stained glass. The simple elegance of the chapel's plan and exterior belie the wonders within: slender fan-vaulting soars overhead – surely one of the most impressive feats of ceiling-making in the western world – seeming to sprout organically from the walls, the whole space illuminated by a brilliant array of 16th-century stained glass windows, thankfully spared by the 17th-century iconoclasts. Construction on the chapel began in 1446 at the instigation of Henry VI, the centrepiece of his grand project for the University, and was completed by Henry VIII, taking over 100 years to construct. The altarpiece at the east end of the simple rectangular plan is Rubens' *Adoration of the Magi*. The chapel's other pride and joy is its world-famous boys' choir, which can be heard in action at choral evensong most afternoons during term-time, as well as at the internationally popular Christmas carol service.

Continuing south a few yards down King's Parade, along the city's main tourist drag, the little church tucked up **St Bene't** Street is the oldest in Cambridge, with a Saxon tower and arch, originally the chapel of **Corpus Christi College**, which is next up on the left. The Old Court of Corpus is the earliest college 'quad' in existence, built shortly after the foundation of the college in 1352. The playwright and contemporary of Shakespeare **Christopher Marlowe** began Cambridge's reputation for educating future spies here in the 16th century and a portrait of someone that could well be the man himself hangs in the college hall.

Opposite Corpus is **St Catharine's College**, known as 'Cats', with an attractive 18th-century brick courtyard. Behind, down Silver Street or King's Lane, is **Queens' College**, founded as Queen's by the wife of Henry VI in 1448, rechristened and endowed by the wife of Edward VI (hence the relocated apostrophe). One of the smallest and prettiest colleges in the city to look at, it provided lodgings in the Pump Court tower for the great Humanist Erasmus who saved the University's academic reputation throughout Europe in 1511 by bringing the teaching of Greek to England. The combination of Queens' red-brick Tudor buildings – Gatehouse, Cloister Court and President's Lodge – is charming. Crossing the Cam, but best seen from Silver Street, is the **Mathematical Bridge**, a much-restored 18th-century design. Heading down to the river, Mill Lane is the most popular place in the city to hire a punt, near the Doubletree hotel or the Mill pub; see What to do, page 81.

Back on Trumpington Street, the continuation of King's Parade, on the left is **Pembroke College**, with a fine classical chapel designed by Wren – his first major church project no less. The college has a long list of famous alumni, including Pitt the Younger – Prime Minister at the age of 23 – the poets Edmund Spenser and Ted Hughes, and comedian Peter Cook. Opposite Pembroke is **Peterhouse**, the smallest and oldest college in the University, founded by the Bishop of Ely in 1281. The college hall remains much as it was when built, while its well-kept garden and pretty octagonal courtyard are also worth a peek. Tom Sharpe's satirical novel *Porterhouse Blue* was based on Peterhouse. The Fitzwilliam Museum (see below) is next door.

The museums

Thanks to the University, for a market town Cambridge is blessed with an unusually large and well-endowed collection of museums, at least 10 in total. Next door to Peterhouse stands their flagship, the grand neoclassical façade of the **Fitzwilliam Museum** ⓘ *Trumpington St, T01223-332900 www.fitzmuseum.cam.ac.uk, Tue-Sat 1000-1700, Sun and bank holiday Mon 1200-1700, free*, without doubt one of the best reasons to visit the city in the first place. Founded in 1816, it houses a host of antiquities from Ancient Egypt, Greece and Rome, as well as applied arts from sculpture and furniture to clocks and rugs, alongside precious manuscripts and an outstanding collection of Old Master paintings, drawings and prints. Be sure to look up as you pass beneath its grand portico to enjoy its extraordinary gem-like Victorian coffered ceiling. Highlights of the collection on display in the magnificent Founder's Building include paintings by Titian, Vernonese, Rubens, Canaletto, Hogarth, Reynolds, Stubbs, Modigliani, Renoir, Cezanne and Picasso; Breughel's *A Vase of Flowers*, Monet's *Poplars*, and Vecchio's *Venus and Cupid*.

Back past Peterhouse and a right turn up Pembroke Street brings you into the heart of the University's scientific and museum quarter. First on the left is the **Whipple Museum of the History of Science** ⓘ *Free School La, T01223-330906, www.hps.cam.ac.uk, Mon-Fri 1230-1630, free*, housed in an Elizabethan hall and featuring historic scientific instruments, apparatus and photography. Highlights include the Grand Orrery, an astronomical model made by George III's instrument maker, George Adams, as well as displays of scientific instruments from the Middle Ages to the present day.

Close by in Downing Street, is the **University Museum of Zoology** ⓘ *New Museums Site, Downing St, T01223-336650, www.museum.zoo.cam.ac.uk, Mon-Fri 1000-1645, Sat 1100-1600, free*, displaying a wide array of recent and fossilized skeletal animals, including a huge whale, and an almost comprehensive display of stuffed British birds. There is also a permanent exhibition of specimens collected by Charles Darwin on his famous voyage on the *Beagle*.

Over the road is the **Museum of Archaeology and Anthropology** ⓘ *T01223-333516, maa.cam.ac.uk, Tue-Sat 1030-1630, free*. It holds important archaeological collections from palaeolithic Europe, Asia and Africa, pre-Columbian South America and early Mediterranean civilizations and anthropological collections from the South Seas and Northwest America, including the inevitable totem pole, as well as lots of interesting photographs, textiles, canoes and masks.

Next door is the **Sedgwick Museum of Earth Sciences** ⓘ *T01223-333456,www.sedgwickmuseum.org, Mon-Fri 0900-1300, 1400-1700, Sat 1000-1600, free*, the oldest museum in the University, where you are greeted by a full-size (5.5 m) model of an iguanodon. Highlights include the colourful mineral collection, and also some 250 million-year-old fossilized lightning, looking like a miniature volcano (about 6 cm across) from prehistoric beaches on the isle of Arran. It also has displays on the solar system and local geology, including the Fens.

A right turn south at the end of Downing Street, onto St Andrews Street, and a half-mile walk arrives at the **Scott Polar Research Institute** ① *Lensfield Rd, T01223-336540, www.spri.cam.ac.uk, Tue-Sat 1000-1600, free,* founded in 1920 in memory of Captain Scott's ill-fated expedition to the South Pole. The recently redeveloped Polar Museum, divided into Arctic and Antarctic galleries, includes maps, journals, photographs and equipment related to polar exploration past and present.

A few hundred yards further on down Hills Road and right onto Bateman Street is the **University Botanic Garden** ① *1 Brookside, T01223-336265, www.botanic.cam.ac.uk, daily Apr-Sep daily 1000-1800, Feb, Mar and Oct closes at 1700, Nov-Jan closes at 1600, £4.50, under-16s free,* a plant-lovers paradise in a formal garden with greenhouses. There's also a great little café with free Wi-Fi and a shop.

The Backs

As the location of Peterhouse suggests, the University was founded between the High Street (now Trinity Street, King's Parade and Trumpington Street) and what was once called Milne Street (now only surviving as Trinity Lane and Queen's Lane) which ran alongside the river. Until the 18th century, 'the backs' of colleges like King's, Clare, Trinity and St John's overlooked busy coal and corn wharves. Now the view could hardly be more different. The Backs are one of the city's most celebrated assets, beautiful green lawns, playing fields and meadows, ablaze with flowers in the spring, strung together with charming old stone bridges crossing the Cam into college gardens. Their leafy extent can easily be viewed by cars or bikes crawling along the congested Queen's Road, but can only be fully appreciated by walkers and especially by punters. **Punting** could almost have been invented for the purpose of idling away a few hours here floating past some of the most beautiful old buildings in England. That's no secret though, which can mean that the footpaths are sometimes less crowded than the water. Private footpaths across the Backs head straight over the bridges into the colleges, open whenever the colleges are. Punts can be hired from Silver Street, Granta Place, Garret Hostel Lane or Magdalene Bridge (see What to do, page 81). Granta Place on Mill Lane is the most popular, because here you have the choice of either heading upriver towards Grantchester, or downriver through the Backs. What the Grantchester way lacks in architectural wonder it makes up for in delightful pastoral stretches, with cows ruminating on Coe Fen.

North of Market Hill

Back in the centre of town in the market square, a right turn on **Trinity** Street leads past the street's eponymous college, the University's largest (with over 600 undergraduates) and grandest. In fact it's a union of two old colleges, Michaelhouse and King's Hall, amalgamated by Henry VIII. At about two acres, its Great Court is also the most spacious of all Oxbridge quads, made famous in the film *Chariots of Fire* for the Great Court Run. A traditional wacky race in which undergraduates in full evening dress after a heavy supper try to complete a circuit of the court in the time it takes for the clock to strike midnight. It's only been successfully achieved once, by Lord Burghley in the early 1920s, an ancestor of Queen Elizabeth I's chancellor. During her reign, the oldest part of the Court was built using stones from the old Grey Friars monastery which stood where Sidney Sussex now stands. The college's other highlight is its magnificent Wren library, along the west side of Nevile's Court. Two decades or so before it was built Isaac Newton was up at Trinity, in 1661. (He published *Principia Mathematica* in 1687 after being made Professor of Mathematics and allegedly hit on the head by an apple.) Other celebrated Trinity alumni include Lord Byron, who famously kept a bear in his rooms, Wittgenstein, Nabokov, the spies Philby, Burgess and Blunt, and Prince Charles.

Trinity Lane twists down the south side of the college towards the Backs, and the front door of **Clare College**, tucked behind the Old Schools. With its austere and beautiful 'Carolean' buildings dating from the 1640s, part of the Classical Revival, and one of the University's most beautiful gardens, it's well worth a look around, as is the very fine **Clare Bridge**, with its stone balls balanced on its parapet. As a jolly jape, undergraduates apparently replaced one of them with a polystyrene replica, nonchalantly toppling it off onto a terrified punt-load of tourists beneath.

Beyond Trinity is **St John's College**, the second largest in the University, founded by Bishop Fisher, who was martyred in the same year as Sir Thomas More under Henry VIII. Along with its fine Tudor gateway, the college has some of the most extraordinary buildings in the city, including its hammer-beamed hall, beautiful Tudor Second Court, and Combination Room, with a spectacular panelled gallery and ornate plaster ceiling. The College also has some of the most beautiful and immaculately kept gardens. The neo-Venetian **Bridge of Sighs** makes a picturesque river crossing from the college.

St John Street, as Trinity Street has become, ends at the junction of Bridge Street and Sydney Street, where stands the **Round Church of the Holy Sepulchre** ① *Bridge St, T01223-311602, http://christianheritage.org.uk, Mon-Sat 1000-1700, Sun 1300-1700, £1.50, under-15s free, 1½-hr guided walks Thu at 1100 and Sun at 1430, £6, £4 full-time students.* As its name suggests, this unusual round church was based on the one in Jerusalem, and now houses a Christian visitor centre offering guided city tours and a video on Cambridge history. It's one of only five round churches in England, founded by the Knights Templar.

A left turn onto Bridge Street leads down to the river and **Magdalene Bridge** and **Quayside**, a pleasant pedestrianized riverside spot for a drink outdoors at one of the bars here. A boardwalk runs to the right along the river from here to Jesus Green, passing the old monastic buildings of Magdalene College. The river here is always busy with punts and chauffeur-punt touts in high season. Over the river on the left-hand side, the **Cambridge and County Folk Museum** ① *Castle St, T01223-355159, www.folk museum.org.uk, Tue-Sat 1030-1700, Sun and bank holiday Mon 1400-1700, £3, concessions £2, 1 child free with every paying adult, otherwise £1,* is housed in an old pub with eight different displays on various facets of local history, including domestic crafts, fens and folklore, and also the University and the City. A few yards up the road is more sophisticated local operation, **Kettle's Yard** ① *Castle St, T01223-748100, www.kettlesyard.co.uk, house Tue-Sun and bank holiday Mon 1400-1700 (1600 in winter), gallery Tue-Sun and bank holiday Mon 1130-1700, free.* Founded in 1957, the house contains artworks by the likes of Ben Nicholson, Barbara Hepworth, Brancusi and the St Ives School, including Alfred Wallis. There are changing exhibitions of contemporary art. The gallery also holds chamber music concerts but the music programme is being put on hold until autumn 2013 due to building work, so Kettles Yard will only be organizing lunchtime concerts to be held across the road in St Giles Church on Fridays from 1300 to 1340, free but donations welcome.

Ten-to-three?

The image of Cambridge that has proved most enduring remains that surrounding the short, beautiful life of the poet Rupert Brooke before the First World War. His famous lines from 'The Old Vicarage, Grantchester', "Stands the church clock at ten-to-three/ And is there honey still for tea?" have come to epitomize the university and its gilded youth's immortal charms. The persistence of this sentimental picture of the place was guaranteed by his death aged 27 on board a troopship bound for Gallipoli in April 1915. He was buried in an olive grove on the Greek island of Skyros, giving the stamp of truth to his other equally famous lines: "If I should die, think only this of me:/That there's some corner of a foreign field/That is forever England".

A right turn onto Sydney Street from Bridge Street heads south again, towards **Sidney Sussex**, Oliver Cromwell's college, with a dissenting chapel orientated north-south. Just before it Jesus Lane leads off to the left. **Jesus College** was founded in 1496 by another Bishop of Ely on the site of the St Radegund's nunnery. Its Cloister Court was created by improving the nunnery's cloisters and its chapel is equally ancient, with some fine stained glass by the Arts and Crafts movement. Opposite the college stands the outstanding but neglected Victorian church of **All Saints'**. Beyond to the north are the green acres of **Jesus Green** and **Midsummer Common**, attractive places to take a picnic or go for a walk beside the river.

Around Cambridge

A couple of miles southwest of the city centre, best reached by a leisurely stroll or punt along the Cam, is **Grantchester**, the epicentre of the Rupert Brooke cult that contributed so much to Cambridge's image between the wars. The Old Vicarage, where the poet stayed while at the university, is now the home of politician and novelist Jeffrey Archer. The church clock doesn't still stand at 10 to three (see box, above) although there could well be honey for tea, or a refreshing pint in one of several pubs in the village. **Trumpington**, a mile away, is an even more charming, well-kept little village, less mobbed by day trippers.

Six miles south of Trumpington, near Junction 10 of the M11, the **Imperial War Museum** ① *Duxford, T01223-835000, www.iwm.org.uk, Mid-Mar to Oct 1000-1800, Nov to mid-Mar 1000-1600, £17.50, concessions £14, under-16s free*, has one of the finest collections of antique and modern military aircraft in the world, with about 150 of the things in vast hangars with an American Air Museum SR71 Blackbird spy-plane, the B24 bomber, a flight simulator and also a land warfare museum full of frightening tanks and things in their natural habitat. There's a Battle of Britain exhibition and in AirSpace, which shows the story of British and Commonwealth aviation, there is a Spitfire, Lancaster bomber and Concorde. There are four air shows in 2013, in May, July, September and October; see the website for details.

A mile southeast of Trumpington the **Gog Magog hills** are named after the legendary giants slain by the ancient British King Brute. Hardly giants themselves, the 90-m hills still provide good views over the surrounding flatlands, as does **Wandlebury** Iron Age hill fort next door, surrounded by 40 ha of woodland, which is a great place for a picnic and a walk.

Five miles further on down the A1307, **Linton Zoo** ① *Hadstock Rd, Linton, T01223-891308, www.lintonzoo.co.uk, daily 1000-1800 (closing at 1700 Apr, May Sep Oct), Nov-Mar 1030-1600, £9, £8 concessions, 2-13 years olds £6.50,* is famous for its big cats, a well-managed zoo with giant tortoises and other exotic species in about 6.5 ha.

Ely and the Fens

The Fens stretch out north of Cambridge and west of Breckland – a completely flat, oddly depressing area of rich farmland divided up by drainage ditches and dykes. One of the earliest entirely man-made and hence industrialized landscapes in Europe, the area was once a mysterious and inaccessible tract of marshland dotted with gravelly little islands. These provided safe havens in the east from Neolithic times right up to the 17th century and the accomplishment of the first serious drainage scheme. Down the ages they attracted a variety of colourful characters, from monks, monarchs and hermits to outlaws, traitors and poets. The most striking survivor from those times is Ely, best approached through fenland mists, when its extraordinary cathedral and octagonal lantern loom ahead, floating on a rise in the ground in the distance. The Isle of Ely, named after all the delicious eels that once squirmed round its shores, still boasts very little other than its beautiful cathedral, marooned in modern East Anglia as surely as it was once in marshland.

Visiting Ely and the Fens

Getting there A surprisingly important **rail** junction for a place of its size, Ely can be reached direct from Liverpool, Norwich, London and Cambridge. The station is about five minutes' walk from the centre. Ely is about 20 minutes north of Cambridge up the A10. **Buses** run to Ely from King's Lynn and Cambridge. ›› *See Transport, page 81.*

Getting around Although there is a local bus network, a car or bike are easily the best ways of exploring the Fens.

Tourist information Ely TIC ① *29 St Mary's St, T01353-662062, visitely.eastcambs.gov.uk, Apr-Oct daily 1000-1700, Nov-Mar Mon-Fri and Sun 1100-1600, Sat 1000-1700.*

Background

Ely was effectively founded by a seventh-century Northumbrian Queen on the run. Etheldreda was fleeing her husband Egfrid, whom she had denied any sexual favours for 12 years in order to maintain a vow of chastity. She was so pious that she founded a monastery here (in 673) and blamed the throat infection that finally killed her on her necklace. Known locally as St Audrey, in her honour the townsfolk took to wearing lace in Tudor times instead of jewellery, some of it so cheap and showy that it gave us the word 'tawdry'. Between times, Ely also became famous as the site of the last stand against the Normans of the outlaw Hereward the Wake. William the Conqueror tried unsuccessfully to oust him and his gang of Danes several times by building pontoon causeways across the marshes from the village of Aldreth. Belsar's Hill, near the village of Willingham, was the site of one of the Conqueror's wooden siege forts. Hereward was finally betrayed by the monks, who provided William with local information and were heavily fined for their trouble. Since those days, because of its peculiar position, it has retained a remarkable number of medieval and Tudor buildings, many now attractive restaurants and teashops.

Places in Ely

One of the most beautiful examples of its kind in the country, **Ely Cathedral** ① *Chapter House, The College, T01353-667735, www.elycathedral.org, Apr-Oct daily 0700-1830, Nov-Mar Mon-Sat 0700-1830, Sun 0700-1730, services Sun 0815, 1030 and 1600, week days 0730, 0800, 1210 (Thu) and 1730, admission including a tour £7.50, concessions £6.50, children free, admission with Octagon or West Tower £14, concessions £13 (children aged 10 and over only are allowed up the towers)*, was rebuilt by the Normans. In the 14th century it was embellished with the inspiring octagonal tower that can be seen for many miles around on a clear day. This beautiful Gothic structure was designed and built by one of the greatest of medieval architects, local monk Alan de Walsingham. In Febuary 1322, as the brothers were retiring to bed, the old Norman tower collapsed. Alan rushed out to survey the ruins, and swore with God's help to 'set his hand to work'. The Lady Chapel has the broadest medieval vaulted ceiling in the country. In the Treforium, the **Stained Glass Museum** ① *T01353-660347, www.stainedglassmuseum.org, same as the cathedral, see above, £4, under-16s free*, contains over a hundred examples of coloured glass dating from 1200. They are also run day-long workshops on making it.

Relocated to the Old Gaol in 1997, the local history **museum** ① *Market St, T01353-666655, www.elymuseum.org.uk, Apr-Sep Mon-Sat 1030-1700, Sun 1300-1700, Nov-Mar Mon and Wed-Sat 1030-1600, Sun 1300-1600, £3.50, under-16s £1*, does a good job of filling the background, with the usual fossils, prehistoric weapons, Roman and Anglo-Saxon finds, as well as an exhibition on the treatment of the Cambridgeshire Regiment as POWs by the Japanese during the Second World War. There are also displays on the Fens and its geography, social history and agriculture.

Around Ely

The National Trust **Wicken Fen** ① *T01353-720274, www.nationaltrust.org.uk, daily dawn to dusk, Fen Cottage Mar-Oct Wed 1100-1500, Sat-Sun 1400-1700, except summer holidays Wed-Sun 1100-1700, Cycle hire Apr-Oct Sat-Sun 1000-1700, £5.90, under-16s £2.95*, is one of Europe's most important wetlands and one of the last surviving pieces of the wilderness that once covered most of East Anglia but have now been replaces by arable farmland. It has a restored Fen Cottage showing how life was in the early 20th century and the last working windpump in the Fens. You can explore the fen by following one of the boardwalks or many trails, hiring a bike or taking a boat trip along Wicken Lode. There is also a visitor centre, café and shop. The restored **Stretham Old Engine** ① *T01353-648578, www.stretham oldengine.org.uk, Mar-Sep twice a month, call or see the website for dates 1330-1700, £3, under-16s £1*, has an impressive land-drainage beam steam engine put in place in 1831 to pump out the fen when it flooded, a job previously done far less effectively by windmills.

Six miles north of Cambridge is **Anglesey Abbey** ① *Quy Rd, Lode, T01223-8100080, www.nationaltrust.org.uk, check website or call for opening times, house and gardens £10.40, gardens only £6.35*, which is not actually an abbey, but a former priory turned into a country house. It's set in 40 ha of formal landscaped gardens with a restored working water mill, which produces flour for sale at the abbey. There's also a great new giant treehouse.

Cambridge listings

◉ Where to stay

For hotel and restaurant price codes and other relevant information, see pages 9-12.

Cambridge and around *p67, map p68*
Accommodation in central Cambridge is expensive. There are plenty of B&Bs on the outskirts, some of the best along Milton Rd, and also in Chesterton Rd. Given that the nightlife is hardly jumping, though, it might be as good to go for better value rooms in one of the villages just outside town, many with regular and reliable bus services to and from the city.

££££ Doubletree by Hilton Cambridge, Granta Pl, Mill La, T01223-259988, www.doubletreecambridge.com. The smartest hotel in the city and in a beautiful location by the river only 5 mins' walk from the centre. It has a lovely terrace bar and brasserie backing onto the punt-crammed Cam, as well as spacious, comfortable rooms with river views. Indoor heated pool, gym, sauna, steam room and bicycle hire. Formerly called the **Garden House Hotel**.

££££ Hotel du Vin, Trumpington St, T01223-227330, www.hotelduvin.com. Centrally located hotel in a former university building, with original architectural features, superbly decorated rooms, a library and a cellar bar. The restaurant (**££**) serves great food. Recommended.

££££-£££ Hotel Felix, Huntingdon Rd, T01223-277977, www.hotelfelix.co.uk. Located about a mile north of the centre, easily accessible by bus or a 30-min walk, this stylish hotel has attractive gardens and rooms with contemporary decor. The restaurant serves excellent food, including award-winning breakfast which is included in the rate. Free Wi-Fi and parking. Recommended.

£££ Arundel House Hotel, 53 Chesterton Rd, T01223-367701, www.arundelhouse hotels.co.uk. Terraced Victorian traditional hotel overlooking the river Cam and Jesus Green only 5 mins' walk to the centre. There's a reasonable menu in the restaurant.

£££ Cambridge City Hotel, Downing St, T01223-464491, www.cambridgecity hotel.co.uk. Thoroughly modern and upholstered city centre option, located right next to the main shopping area. It's popular with corporate clients as well as tourists.

£££ Cambridge Rooms, www.cambridgerooms.co.uk. Stay in one of Cambridge's centrally located historic colleges in a student room during the holidays. Breakfast is included.

£££ Duke House, 1 Victoria St, T01223-314773, http://dukehouse cambridge.co.uk. Lovely B&B with beautifully decorated rooms a short walk from the centre. Free Wi-Fi and limited parking available.

££ City Roomz, Station Rd, T01223-304050, www.cityroomz.com. Clean and comfortable budget option in a converted granary 50 m from the station.

££ Springfield House, 16 Horn La, Linton, T01223-891383, www.springfieldhouse.org. Gorgeous B&B in a Victorian schoolhouse with beautifully kept gardens next to the River Granta, worth the trek out to this village 10 miles away from Cambridge. In summer, breakfast is served in the conservatory with a mimosa tree. There's a bus service into Cambridge.

£ Cambridge YHA, 97 Tenison Rd, T0845-371 9728, www.yha.org.uk. Close to the station, a Victorian townhouse about 15 mins' walk from the centre with 108 beds in 2-8 bedded rooms. Booking well in advance advisable.

Ely and the Fens *p75*
£££ Cathedral House, 17 St Mary's St, Ely, T01353-662124, www.cathedralhouse.co.uk.

Large rooms, a walled garden and also very close to the cathedral. Free Wi-Fi and parking.

£££ The Lamb Hotel, 2 Lynn Rd, Ely, T01353-663574, www.oldenglishinns.co.uk. Part of the Old English Inns chain, perfectly comfortable in a slightly bland sort of way and very close to the cathedral. Free W-Fi.

£££ The Old Hall, Stuntney, T01353-663275, www.theoldhallely.co.uk. Just a mile from Ely is this handsome country house set in formal gardens offering B&B accommodation in sumptuously decorated rooms, some with views of Ely Cathedral.

£££ Sycamore House, 91 Cambridge Rd, Ely, T01353-662139, www.sycamore guesthouse.co.uk. Very comfortable B&B, but a 10-min walk from town. The large garden overlooks the Ely golf course.

££ The Old Vicarage, Isleham, T01638-780095, www.oldvicarage isleham.co.uk. Nine miles from Ely towards Newmarket is this B&B in a 19th-century vicarage set in peaceful gardens.

❶ Restaurants

Cambridge and around p67, map p68
For pub grub, see also the Pubs, bars, and clubs section, as many Cambridge pubs serve good-value dishes. If you're looking for budget places to eat, head to Mill Road, across Parker's Piece, about 10 mins' walk southeast of the centre. Choose from sustainable fish at the award-winning **Sea Tree** fish and chip shop (http://theseatree.co.uk) on the Broadway, authentic Brazilian fare at **Café Brazil** or North African cuisine at **Bedouin** (www.bedouin-cambridge.com). There's also great coffee, roasted on site, at **Hot Numbers** (http://hotnumberscoffee.co.uk) at Dales Brewery, Gwydir St, just off Mill Rd.

£££ Midsummer House, Midsummer Common, T01223-369299. Universally acknowledged to be the best (and most expensive) restaurant in town, with 2 Michelin stars, but it deserves all the praise.

Innovative and delicious gourmet cuisine is served up with unfailing attention to detail in a delightful conservatory and garden, with a balcony area overlooking the Cam. Booking essential. Recommended.

££ 22 Chesterton Rd, 22 Chesterton Rd, T01223-351880, www.restaurant22.co.uk. Quite staid, classy joint but with a surprisingly innovative menu served up in an Edwardian dining room. Set 3-course meals are £33.95. Best to book in advance.

££ Fitzbillies, Trumpington St, T01223-352500, www.fitzbillies.com. Open daily for lunch and Thu, Fri and Sat for dinner. Until a few years ago this was a long-established and well-respected bakery, which has now been taken over by food writer Tim Hayward. Luckily, he's retained the elegant wooden front windows dating from the 1920s. Their famous sticky Chelsea buns are particularly delicious and available to send anywhere in the world by mail order, and there are plenty of other tempting treats on offer for lunch and dinner.

££ Loch Fyne Oysterhouse, 37 Trumpington St, T01223-362433, www.lochfyne-restaurants.com. In the middle of town opposite Peterhouse College, this is a fine example of the reliable national seafood chain doing very fresh fish in cheerful and easy-going surroundings. Good-value 2-course menu for £9.95.

£ Adilia's Norfolk St Bakery, Norfolk St, T01223-660163. Like Fitzbillies, this newly opened place had been a bakery for many years (since 1868) but has been reborn with a Portuguese influence thanks to its owner, Adilia. Make sure you try the fantastic Portuguese custard tarts and organic sourdough.

£ Bill's, Green St, T01223-329638. www.bills-website.co.uk. Great café serving good-value dishes, including breakfasts, with lots of vegetarian options. Service can be a bit slow when they're busy and you may have to share a table.

£ Cocum Restaurant, Castle Hill, T01223-366668, www.cocumrestaurant.co.uk. Excellent Keralan curry restaurant at the top of Castle Hill, about 10 mins from the centre but worth the walk up the hill.

£ Michaelhouse Café, Trinity St, T01223-309147, www.michaelhousecafe.co.uk. Closed Sun. Good café located in a 14th-century church near Trinity and Kings colleges, run by food writer Bill Sewell. Great coffee and homemade cakes too. Recommended.

£ Rainbow Café, 9a King's Parade, T01223-321551, www.rainbowcafe.co.uk. A long-established and popular vegetarian restaurant tucked away in a basement location right on the main tourist drag opposite Kings College.

£ Varsity Restaurant, 35 St Andrew's St, T01223-356060, www.varsityrestaurant.co.uk. A Greek and Mediterranean restaurant which has been around for years and remains popular for its cheap and cheerful approach.

Ely and the Fens *p75*

££ The Boathouse, 5-5a Annesdale, Ely, T01353-664388, www.cambscuisine.com. Owned by the same company as **The Cambridge Chophouse** and the brilliant **The Cock** in Hemingford Grey, near St Ives, this riverside gastro pub is in a great spot overlooking the Ouse, 10 mins' walk from the Cathedral. They serve superb food, including their own homemade sausages.

££ Old Fire Engine House, 25 St Mary's, T01353-662582, www.theoldfireengine house.co.uk. A welcoming place that has been around for years and some think it shows, but it remains the smartest option in town. Dishes on the traditional menu feature locally sourced ingredients.

£ Montaz, 39-41 Market St, Ely, T01353-669930, www.montaz.co.uk. The best curry house in Ely.

£ Peacocks Tearoom, 65 Waterside, Ely, T01353-661100, www.peacocks tearoom.co.uk. Tea rooms don't come much better than this award-winning one in a lovely old building next to the river. Choose from a huge range of teas (over 70 different types), perfectly served in dainty tea cups with a great choice of homemade cakes or scones. Lunches are also served, including soup with freshly made cheese scones. Recommended.

🎵 Pubs, bars and clubs

Cambridge and around *p67, map p68*

The Cambridge Blue, Gwydir St, T01223-471680, www.the-cambridge blue.co.uk. An eccentric drinking hole named after the colour sports teams from Cambridge University wear, with great ales, a conservatory and good bar food. Recommended.

The Eagle, Bene't St, T01223-505020. A rambling, pine-panelled atmospheric pub, one of the oldest in Cambridge, with famous 'RAF ceiling' scribbled on during the Second World War by locally based British and American airmen. Its claim to fame is that the scientists James Watson and Francis Crick first publicly announced their discovery of DNA here, an event commemorated on a plaque outside the pub. Recommended.

The Elm Tree, 16a Orchard St, T01223-502632, theelmtreecambridge.co.uk. This small backstreet local and microbrewery sells its own real ales as well as Belgian beers, fruit wines, ciders and perrys.

Fort St George, next to Midsummer House on Midsummer Common, T01223-354327. A good spot for a beer in summer, with outside seating on the river beside the boathouses.

Free Press, Prospect Row, T01223-368337, www.freepresspub.com. Near Christ's Piece, just round the corner from **The Elm Tree**, is another small real ale pub, in an old terraced house with an attractive little garden. Also does good bar food.

The Granta, 14 Newnham Rd, T01223-505016, http://gkpubs.co.uk. Great location with a beer garden overlooking a mill pond edged by willow trees, a lovely stroll across the meadows by the river from the centre. Barbecue dishes available in summer. A handily placed punting station is right next to the pub, see page 81.

Kingston Arms, 33 Kingston St, off Mill Rd, T01223-319414, www.kingston-arms.co.uk. Popular local with a good choice of real ales and award-winning excellent pub food.

The Mitre, 17 Bridge St, T01223-358403, www.nicholsonspubs.co.uk. Atmospheric pub near the Round Church.

Ely and the Fens p75

The Maltings Arts Centre, Ely, T01353-669757, http://themaltingsely.com. Restaurant closed Oct-spring, bar open year round. This arts centre has a decent wine bar and brasserie on the Great Ouse's waterfront to go with its cinema and theatre.

The Plough, Little Downham, T01353-698297. Winner of CAMRA's rural pub in Ely of 2012, this friendly local a mile from Ely has good real ales and serves Thai food 6 days a week.

⚙ Entertainment

Cambridge and around p67, map p68

Student amusement abounds during term time, with bands and drinking sessions, along with post-exam hysteria in May/Jun. Try also www.visitcambridge.org.

Film, theatre and music

ADC Theatre, Park St, T01223-300085, www.adctheatre.com. The University of Cambridge's own theatre, run by students and staging varied performances in drama, dance and music. It helped to launch the careers of acclaimed actors such as Emma Thompson and Sir Ian McKellen.

Arts Picture House, St Andrews St, T0871-902 5720, www.picturehouses.co.uk. 3-screen general release art house films.

Arts Theatre, St Edward's Passage, T01223-503333, https://cambridgearts theatre.purchase-tickets-online.co.uk. Regional theatre with an excellent reputation, which stages top-quality dance, music, drama and pantomime shows.

Cambridge Corn Exchange, Wheeler St, T01223-357851, www.cornex.co.uk. This is the city's principal venue for larger touring productions, including opera, dance and live music.

The Junction, Clifton Rd, T01223-511511, www.junction.co.uk. Club nights, comedy and live music.

Kettle's Yard, see page 73. For intimate classical and folk concerts.

Mumford Theatre, East Rd, T01223-352932, www.anglia.ac.uk. Part of the Anglia Ruskin University campus, this university theatre features performances by students and community and touring theatre companies.

⚙ Festivals

Cambridge and around p67, map p68

Mid-Mar Cambridge Science Week, www.cam.ac.uk/sciencefestival. With lectures and other science-related events.

May Cambridge Beer Festival, www.cambridgebeerfestival.com. Held on Jesus Green, usually during the penultimate week in May. There is also a Cambridge Winter Ale Festival, held in late Jan and a smaller Cambridge Octoberfest, both held at the University Social Club, Mill Lane.

Jun May Week, in the middle of Jun has student balls, japes and general hilarity to celebrate the end of exams.

Jun Strawberry Fair, www.strawberry-fair.org.uk. A full-on hippy trippy long-running free festival on Midsummer Common, held on the first Sat in Jun.

Jul Cambridge Folk Festival, near the end of the month, www.cambridgefolk festival.co.uk. Booking essential for one of the world's first and most prestigious 4-day folk music festivals. One day as well as weekend camping tickets available.

Jul-Aug Cambridge Shakespeare Festival, www.cambridgeshakespeare.com. An outdoor festival with performances taking place in the gardens of a variety of colleges.

Sep Cambridge Film Festival, www.cambridgefilmfestival.org.uk. Well-respected festival featuring visiting famous filmmakers (including the likes of Wim Wenders, Michael Winterbottom and Terry Gilliam) and outdoor screenings at locations such as Jesus Green Lido and Granchester Meadows.

▲ What to do

Cambridge and around *p67, map p68*
Punting
Granta Canoe and Punt, Newnham Rd, next to the Granta pub, T01223-301845, http://puntingincambridge.com. Winter guided punt tours only, early spring and late autumn daily 1100-1700, May-Sep 0900-dusk. Canoes and punts £18 per hour.
Scudamore's Punting Company, Granta Pl, Mill La, T01223-359750, www.scudamores.com. Mar-Oct 0900-dusk, Nov-Feb Sat, Sun only 1000-dusk. £20 an hour. In high season, expect to queue if you want a punt any time after 1300. Choose either an upriver boat, for Coe Fen and the 3-hr round-trip to Grantchester from their Mill La boatyard near the Doubletree hotel, or a downriver boat for the Backs and the 2-hr, 2-mile round-trip to Jesus Green Lock, from their boatyard between the Anchor on Silver St and the Mill pub on Mill La. The upriver boats and the stretches of river they ply are generally less busy and more rural than the downriver ones. There is a third boatyard next to Magdalene Bridge, near the Quayside area and Caffé Uno.

Swimming pools
Jesus Green Lido, off Chesterton Rd, T01223-302579, www.everyoneactive.com.

A perfect spot on a hot summer's day, this 94-m-long pool is one of the longest in the country, and has a snack bar and grassy areas for picnics.
Parkside Pool, Gonville Pl, T01223-446100, www.everyoneactive.com. The main city swimming pool across Parker's Piece about 10 mins' walk from the centre.

Tours
Walking tours, TIC, see page 67. Daily 2-hr walking tours leave the TIC in Peas Hill at 1100 and 1300 Mon-Sat and at 1300 on Sun and bank holidays. There are extra tours at weekends and in Jul and Aug. Tours cost £17.50, under-16s £8.

Ely and the Fens *p75*
Boat trips
Liberty Belle Riverside Cruises, T07927-390380. Holidays Mon-Fri 1200, Sat-Sun 1100, £5, under-16s £3.50 30-min boatrides along Ely's waterfront in an old river launch from Ship La, in front of the Maltings.

⊖ Transport

Cambridge and around *p67, map p68*
Bicycle
Ben Hayward & Son, 69 Trumpington St, T01223-352294; **Cycle King**, 195 Mill Rd, T01223-212222; **Geoff's Bike Hire**, 65 Devonshire Rd, T01223-365629; **NK Bike Hire**, Cherry Hinton Rd, T01223-505485 and **University Cycles**, 9 Victoria Av, T01223-355517.

Bus
For details of bus travel, contact **Traveline**, T0871-200 2233, http://traveline.info.
Local Cambridge is well served by local buses. The main operator is **Stagecoach**, T01223-423578, www.stagecoachbus.com, which has services to **Ely** (1 hr 25 mins), **Linton**, **Newmarket**, **Saffron Walden**, **Bedford**. Other local companies include **Go Whippet**, T01480-463792,

wwwgowhippet.com, with services north of Cambridge to **Huntingdon** and surrounding towns and villages, and **Myalls**, with services to **Duxford**'s Imperial War Museum on Sun and **Saffron Walden**.

Long distance To **Norwich** (from 2 hrs 40 mins), with **Stagecoach** changing at Newmarket or Bury St Edmunds to a **National Express** coach. The direct service to **Ipswich** (1 hr 15 mins) is run by **National Express**, and departs from Drummer Road coach stop at 1639. They also run the direct hourly service to **London** (1 hr 50 mins) and the regular direct service to **Stansted airport** (1 hr).

Taxi

There are taxi ranks on Drummer St (for the bus station), Emmanuel St, St Andrews St and at the train station.

Train

The main rail perators are **First Capital Connect**, T0844-556 5638, www.firstcapitalconnect.co.uk, and **Northern Rail**, T0844-241 3454, www.northernrail.org. Direct trains from Cambridge to **London King's Cross** (50 mins), or via stations including Royston, Hitchin, Stevenage, Finsbury Park (1 hr 20 mins), and to **London Liverpool St** via stations including Audley End, Bishop's Stortford and Harlow (1 hr 10 mins). There are also regular direct services to **Ely** (15 mins), **Ipswich** (1 hr 20 mins) and **Norwich** (1 hr 20 mins). Trains run direct every hour to **Stansted airport** (30 mins).

❶ Directory

Medical facilities Addenbrooke's, Hills Rd, T01223-245151. www.cuh.org.uk.
Police Parkside Police Station, Parkside, T01223-456111.

Contents

Essex

Essex is the English county that has famously become the butt of many bad jokes, full of 'wannabe' girls and boys ridiculed for their easy virtue, flash consumerism and one-time worship of Margaret Thatcher. In fact, although it may not be very fashionable, Essex conceals some relatively undiscovered countryside within reach of London and many of its villages are just as pretty as those of its more salubrious neighbour, Suffolk. In the east of the county, Uttlesford embraces the three prosperous market towns of Saffron Walden, Thaxted and Great Dunmow. In the west, Colchester is a strange mixed-up kind of place on the site of one of the oldest towns in England and close to the countryside on the river Stour that the painter John Constable committed to canvas in the 19th century. Along the coast, Southend-on-Sea has long been many Eastenders' favourite seaside resort, competing with Clacton-on-Sea further north. Nearby, Frinton-on-Sea is famous for being irredeemably middle class, perhaps in reaction to its neighbours. Beyond is the tidal marshland of Hamford Water, the inspiration for Arthur Ransome's *Swallows and Amazons*.

Saffron Walden, Thaxted, Great Dunmow and around

With the M11 slicing north to Cambridge through its west, the northeast Essex district quaintly entitled Uttlesford embraces the three small towns of Saffron Walden, Thaxted and Great Dunmow. Saffron is the most lively and happening, clustered on a hill beneath its church and castle, close to the stately Jacobean splendour of Audley End House. Little Thaxted's great church, also atop a hill, is the 'Queen of Essex', while the relatively undiscovered countryside south towards the commuter town of Great Dunmow is some of the county's more picturesque. Although too close to the busy sprawl of Stansted Airport for comfort, the ancient tree-filled acres of Hatfield Forest still make for pleasant walking and picnicking. ▶▶ *For listings, see pages 91-92.*

Visiting Saffron Walden, Thaxted and Great Dunmow

Getting there By **train**, Saffron Walden is 1½ miles of Audley End station on the line to Cambridge from London Liverpool Street. Great Dunmow is 8 miles west of Braintree station. By **road**, Saffron Walden is 15 miles south of Cambridge and an hour from London.

Getting around All the towns and villages of the Uttlesford district are tricky to reach by public transport. Unfortunately a car is easily the most convenient way of getting about.

Tourist information Saffron Walden **TIC** ① *Market Place, T01799-524002, www.visitsaffronwalden.gov.uk, Apr-Oct Mon-Sat 0930-1730, Nov-Mar closes at 1700.* **Thaxted Information Centre** ① *7 Town St, T01371-831641. Mar-Oct Thu-Sun 1000-1600 (open at 1230 Fri and 1330 Sun).* **Birchanger Green TIC** ① *Welcome Break Service Station, M11 Junction 8, T01279-508656, Mon-Sat 0930-1730.*

Saffron Walden

Saffron Walden is the prettiest and most lively town in northwest Essex. Originally called Chipping Walden, it became wealthy by growing and trading in saffron crocuses for dyes, medicines and flavouring from the 15th to 18th centuries. The dinky little **Market Square** remains the centre of town, its neoclassical old **Corn Exchange** (now a small library) overlooking market stalls on Tuesday and Saturday and a congested car park the rest of the week. A few steps north of the square, the graceful spire of **St Mary's** (the largest church in Essex) is a useful landmark and Church Street a good place to begin an exploration of the town's warren of gabled, half-timbered streets. The patterned plasterwork on the 15th-century **Sun Inn** is a fine example of the 17th-century art of pargeting. Others can be seen along the High Street and Castle Street, beyond the church, and adjacent to **Bridge End Gardens** ① *open year round, the walled garden and the hedge maze are viewable by appointment with the TIC.* These attractive Victorian formal gardens contain a restored yew hedge maze, pavilions and a kitchen garden. Also on Castle Street, with similar origins to the gardens, is the **Fry Art Gallery** ① *Castle St, T01799-513779, www.fryartgallery.org, Easter-Oct Tue, Thu-Sat 1400-1700, Sat opens at 1100, Sun and bank holidays opens 1415, free, donations suggested,* with its interesting permanent collection of work by eminent local artists, especially the mid-20th century painters and engravers from Great Bardfield, like John Aldridge, Edward Bawden and Eric Ravilious, as well as Marianne Straub and Tom Deakins. At the top end of the street is the **Saffron Walden Museum** ① *Museum St T01799-510333, Mar-Oct Mon-Sat 1000-1700, Sun and bank holidays 1400-1700, Nov-Feb Mon-Sat 1000-1630, Sun and bank holidays 1400-1630, £1.50, concessions 75p, under-16s free,* with the ruins of the town's Norman castle in its grounds. The museum's highlights include a Viking necklace, antique porcelain and the history of saffron as well as plenty to entertain children. A five-minute walk east, on the Common, is the most extensive ancient **turf maze** in Europe – not much to look at but surprisingly tricky to complete.

Audley End House

① *T01799-522842, www.englishheritage.co.uk, Apr-Sep Wed-Sun, bank holidays, grounds 1100-1800, house 1200-1700 (last entries 1 hr before closing), Nov-Mar grounds Sat-Sun and daily Feb half term 1000-1600,. £13, concessions £11,70, children £7.80, grounds only £9, concessions £8.10, children £5.40. Miniature railway, T01799-541354, www.audley-end-railway.co.uk, late Mar to Oct every weekend and school holidays 1200-1645, £4.50, £3.50.*

Half a mile or so west of Saffron Walden, Audley End House is a remarkable Jacobean palace set in lovely landscaped grounds and all the more remarkable because a substantial part of the original house was demolished in the early 18th century. It was built in the early 17th century for the Earl of Suffolk, Lord Treasurer to the indigent James I. (James I supposedly remarked that the house was too big for a King but about right for a Lord Treasurer.) Charles II later bought it as a convenient base from which to enjoy the Sport of Kings – going to the races at Newmarket. As well as the restored Victorian parterre and the ha-ha giving onto rolling green hills dotted with eyecatcher monuments, highlights of the interior are a magnificent carved oak screen in the great hall, an early 18th-century Gothic private chapel, and a string of rooms sumptuously decorated in the 1820s (hung with paintings by Canaletto and Holbein among others). Best of all though is the delicate, painted beauty of the Robert Adam-designed apartments on the ground floor. Friendly well-informed guides are at hand to elucidate each of the rooms' finer points. Also at Audley End, great for the kids, is Lord Braybrooke's **miniature railway** chugging through the woods alongside and over the river Cam for a mile and a half.

Thaxted and around

Thaxted is another picturesque town but much quieter than Saffron, with its fine crumbly medieval Guildhall at the top of the High Street, a cobbled walkway below its flying-buttressed **church** on the hilltop where Holst was organist. Inside, a chapel commemorates John Ball, one of the leaders of the Peasant's Revolt in 1381, and there's lots of medieval stone carving and a beautiful 15th-century stained-glass window of Adam and Eve. The other prominent landmark is the early 19th-century brick-built **windmill** ① *T01371-830285, Easter-Sep Sat, Sun and bank holidays 1400-1600*. Another 5 miles to the east, **Finchingfield** is a pretty little village with a duck pond surrounded by teashops and old pubs, also overlooked by a much smaller church at the top of its hill.

Another six miles east of Thaxted, **Castle Hedingham** ① *T01787-460261, www.hedingham castle.co.uk, call or see the website for opening times, £7.50, under-16s £5*, is quite an impressive Norman keep that has survived since 1140, strongly associated with the De Veres and the Earls of Oxford. The interior will be familiar from many an Errol Flynn movie, featuring a banqueting hall, minstrels gallery and yet another room where Elizabeth I is supposed to have slept. A couple of miles to the east, **Little Maplestead**'s round church is one of only five in England.

Great Dunmow

Uttlesford's third town is Great Dunmow, with much less immediate appeal than Thaxted or Saffron, it is more of a commuter dormitory town though blessed with an attractive rolling green and pond. Just to its northeast, **Little Easton** is a very pretty village with lakeside gardens and an atmospheric church containing marble monuments to the local Maynard family. HG Wells lived here and you can visit the strangely atmospheric **Gardens of Easton Lodge** ① *T01371-876979, www.eastonlodge.co.uk, call or see website for opening times, generally only open 1 Sun a month Apr-Sep plus 2 snowdrop Sun in Feb, £3.50, under-16s free*, a hotch-potch work-in-progress by the Creasey family restoring and adding to Harold Peto's original layout of 1902.

Hatfield Forest

① *T01279-870678, www.nationaltrust.org.uk. Café open Easter-Oct daily 1000-1630, Nov-Easter weekends and school holidays 1000-1530.*
Six miles west of Great Dunmow, off the road to Bishop's Stortford, Hatfield Forest is a medieval royal hunting forest still home to fallow deer, where the woods have been carefully coppiced and pollarded for centuries. Pleasant walks around the grasslands are slightly marred by the air traffic overhead. The long-distance footpath the **Flitch Way** passes through the forest.

Colchester, Constable Country and around

Colchester is and always was an army town. It confidently lays claim to being 'the oldest town in Britain', thanks to a mention by Pliny in AD 77. First known as Camulodunum, meaning 'fortress of the war god Camulos', in pre-Roman days, it is now the base for battalions of the Parachute Regiment, aka the 'Paras'. Possibly also named after Old King Cole, the merry old soul, Colchester is a strange mix of ancient heritage and urban deprivation. Northeast of Colchester, the undeniable charms of Constable Country are milked for all they're worth round Dedham. Several other villages close by, including the painter's birthplace at East Bergholt, are usually less mobbed than the famous Flatford Mill.

Arriving in Colchester
Getting there Trains leave London Liverpool Street every 10 or 20 minutes to Colchester station (45 minutes), operated by **London Midland** (T0844-811 0133, www.londonmidland.com). By **road**, leave London from the east on the A12. Continue northeast on the A12 through Chelmsford, exit A12 at Beacon End on the outskirts of Colchester (1½ hours, 60 miles). **National Express** have services from London Victoria coach station to Colchester bus station, via Stansted Airport (2 hours 20 minutes, or 3 hours 20 minutes via Stansted Airport). ▸▸ *See Transport, page 92.*

Getting around Colchester centre is about a mile square based around the ancient town layout with the River Colne flowing along the north and down the east side. Tendring Peninsula is minutes away from Colchester by car, bus or train, or can easily be cycled via the Wivenhoe Riverside Path.

Tourist information Colchester TIC ① *1 Queen Street, opposite the castle, T01206-282920, www.visitcolchester.com, Mon-Sat 1000-1700.*

Colchester
Okay, so Colchester may not look very Roman today. Even so, with a fair bit of imagination, the original rectangular shape and scale of Camulodunum can still just about be made out. The modern High Street follows the dead straight east–west line of the Roman town laid down over the hill in the first century AD. At its western end, the **Balkerne Gate** was the Romans' entrance from the west, and its remains can still be seen. It looks like a bit of old subway, a short clammy tunnel with a curved brick roof giving onto the A134 rushing past just beneath, but it can claim to be the only surviving Roman gateway in Britain. That fact, along with its age and its setting – in the shadow of the striking bulk of the brick-built Victorian watertower, a hilltop landmark affectionately known as Jumbo, and next to the **Hole in the Wall** pub (aptly named) and Mercury Theatre – make the gate quite a strange and unusual sight.

A beeline east of the gate along Camulodunum's main street passes through the mock-Tudor timber frame of the town's **Post Office** and on to the modern High Street. Half way down the High Street, behind the imposing **Town Hall** with its prominent clocktower, is the **Dutch quarter**, a warren of attractive old streets between West and East Stockwell Streets. **St John's Abbey Gate** ① *www.english-heritage.org.uk, open at any reasonable time,* is all that remains of the vast Benedictine abbey of St John, which was built around 1400.

The substantial remains of the **Norman castle** ① *T01206-282939, closed for major redevelopment until spring 2014*, built on the site of Claudius's temple, using bricks from the Roman town, stand at the top of East Hill, a few hundred yards above the old east gate (long vanished). Set back from the High Street in a pretty park, it was the largest keep ever built by the Normans, between 1076 and 1175, and adapted in the 18th century by the local MP 'for his own personal use', with the addition of large windows, domed tower and tiled roof. The **museum** inside is particularly strong on Roman finds, and medieval life in the town.

Constable Country: the Stour Valley

Northeast of Colchester, the river Stour (usually pronounced 'store') divides Essex from Suffolk and more famously inspired John Constable, one of Britain's greatest landscape painters. Remarkably enough many of the scenes that he made famous, brooded over by his magnificent skies, are still perfectly recognizable today. Dedham is the centre of 'Constable Country', although his birthplace **East Bergholt** and the charming village of **Stoke-by-Nayland**, both just over the border in Suffolk, are in some ways more rewarding places to seek out the picturesque rural idyll of his paintings. The mills of Stratford St Mary also inspired the painter, although today the village is a bit spoiled by the A12. All are in the **Dedham Vale**, a protected AONB (Area of Outstanding Natural Beauty).

Dedham village itself is worth a look though, with its row of grand and carefully preserved Georgian houses lining its main street alongside the 17th-century church. Attractive wooden tiller rowing boats can be hired on the river from here, at **Dedham Boathouse** ① *T01206-323153, http://dedhamboathouse.co.uk, Mar-Sep Sat-Sun, except school holidays when they are available daily 1000-1700, £7 for 30 mins*, on the bridge just outside the village, for a row downstream to Flatford Mill. A 20-minute walk south down a charming narrow alley beside the **Dedham Art and Craft Centre** ① *T01206-322666, www.dedhamartsandcraftcentre.co.uk, daily 1000-1700*, across playing fields and past an extraordinary pink timber-framed Elizabethan courtyard house (*garden open*), brings you to **Castle House** ① *T01206-322127, www.siralfredmunnings.co.uk, Apr-Oct Wed-Sun, bank holidays 1400-1700, £6.50, concessions £5, under-16s £1*. This grand rectory was the home of the quintessentially English portrait painter Sir Alfred Munnings from 1919 until 1959. Most of his portraits involve horse races and country life, and the whole place has a quiet, elegiac atmosphere, a shrine to the historic rural ways of life.

Flatford Mill, the most celebrated of Constable's subjects, featured in several pictures, is just over the border in Suffolk and reached by road through East Bergholt where the church bells are kept in a spooky old wooden cage in the churchyard, apparently because the devil stole the bell tower. Down by the river, the complex of attractions includes a John Constable Exhibition in the thatched **Bridge Cottage** ① *T01206-298260, www.nationaltrust.org.uk, Feb Sat-Sun and Mar and Nov-Dec Wed-Sun 1030-1530, Apr-Oct daily 1000-1700, free*. The **River Stour Trust** ① *T0844-800 5018, every Sun Easter-Oct 10.15-1700, Wed in Aug, regular departures, £5, under-16s £3*, run silent electric launch river trips.

South of Colchester

Two miles south of the town centre, well-signposted, **Bourne Mill** ① *Bourne Rd, Colchester, T01206-572422, www.nationaltrust.org.uk, Easter, May bank holidays, Jun Sun, Jul-Aug Thu and Sun, Sep 14-15 1400-1700, £3, £1.60*, was built as a fishing lodge in 1521, and still has watermill machinery intact inside and out. Also a couple of miles south, on the B1022 towards Maldon, is

Colchester Zoo ① *Maldon Rd, T01206-331292, www.colchester-zoo.com, daily 0930-1730 (or dusk, whichever is earlier), £12.99, under-15s £8.50,* one of the better zoos in England and the home of over 200 species, including rhino, elephants, cheetahs, penguins and seals. The well-designed complex also has adventure playgrounds.

Four miles further south of Colchester on the same road, tucked away down a maze of narrow lanes near Birch, **Layer Marney Tower** ① *T01206-330784, www.layermarney tower.co.uk, end of Mar-Sep Wed and Sun (Jul-Aug also Mon, Tue and Thu) 1200-1700, bank holidays opens at 1100, 1-hr tours second Sun Apr-Sep no extra charge, £7, under-16s £4.50,* is the tallest Tudor gatehouse in the country and quite a surprising find in this relatively out-of-the-way area. Designed in the late 1500s to outdo Hampton Court, its palace was never built. There are fine views from the top.

Essex Coast from Southend to Harwich

There's not a huge amount to recommend the Essex coast apart from its convenience for Londoners. That fact has been quite enough though to ensure that it's still very lively in summer, and it also conceals a few more secluded spots beloved by birdwatchers and oyster-eaters. Southend is the largest seaside resort, a full-on strip of seaside amusements overlooking the longest pier in the world. Further up the coast, succulent Colchester oysters can found at Burnham-on-Crouch and Mersea Island, while the nature reserve at Northey Island in the Blackwater estuary is one of the best for birdwatching within easy reach of the capital. Harwich is the major international North Sea ferry point, with a quaint old town.

Visiting the Essex coast

Getting there   Southend can be reached by **train** from London Fenchurch Street in less than an hour. Trains for Burnham-on-Crouch leave from Liverpool Street and take just over an hour, and to Clacton-on-Sea and Frinton-on-Sea take one hour and 25 minutes. By **road**, Southend is about an hour's drive from central London. Other parts of the coast are easily reached along the A12. Maldon is about 1½ hours from London, Harwich two hours. **National Express** run regular coaches to Southend, Colchester and Harwich from London.

Tourist information Southend TIC ① *Southend Pier, Western Esplanade, T01702-618747, www.visitsouthend.co.uk, Apr-May and Sep-Oct Mon-Fri 0815-1700, Sat-Sun until 1900, May-Sep daily 0815-1900, Nov-Mar daily 0915-1700.* **Clacton TIC** ① *Town Hall, Station Rd, T01255-686633, www.essex-sunshine-coast.org.uk, mid-May to mid-Sep daily 1000-1730, rest of year Mon-Sat 1000-1700.* **Harwich TIC** ① *Iconfield Park, Freshfields Rd, T01255-506139.*

Southend

Southend, the closest seaside resort to the capital, has long been London's East End-on-Sea. Considerably more cheerful than some of its competitors on the opposite bank of the Thames estuary, the 7-mile long beach is surprisingly clean and fronts a south-facing esplanade that still retains some of its Regency splendour if none of its dignity, dominated as it is by loud pubs, fast-food joints and noisy amusement arcades. Younger kids always want to head straight for **Adventure Island** ① *Marine Pde and Western Esplanade, T01702-443400, www.adventureisland.co.uk, daily Easter and end of May to Sep and Sat-Sun May and Sep 1100-1800 (closing between 2000 and 1030 Easter,*

May-Jun and Sep weekends, Oct Sats and summer holidays, half price ride bands after 1800 on these dates), bands for rides from £15 on the day or from £9 online, prices depend on what age rides are suitable for, on the Western Esplanade. The rainy day option is **Sea Life Adventure** ⓘ *Eastern Esplanade, T01702-442200, www.sealifeadventure.co.uk, daily 1000-1700, until 2000 in summer, £9.50 (£7.90 online), under-14s £6.50 (£5.20)*, with an underwater tunnel, crocodiles, piranha tank and turtles. The resort's most famous feature, its **pier** ⓘ *Western Esplanade, T01702-215620, late May-early Sep daily 0815-2000, Apr-May and mid-Sep to Oct Mon-Fri 0815-1800, open until 2000 Sat-Sun, Nov-Mar daily 0915-1700*, is 1.2 miles long, the longest in the world. It is definitely worth the train ride (£3.60 return, under-16s £1.80) or walk along it right out into the estuary, even if the Pavilion and viewpoints at the end are not the most inspiring destination. The pier also has a new cultural centre, which holds regular concerts and exhibitions, with a café and a **museum** ⓘ *Apr-Sep Sun-Wed and bank holidays 1100-1700, £1, under-12s free*.

Southminster peninsula

Seven miles north of Southend as the crow flies (considerably longer by road), **Burnham-on-Crouch** is a popular yachting centre, and makes a good day trip by train from London. Famous for its oysters, it's on the south side of the Southminster peninsula. On the north side, standing in a remote and eerie spot near Bradwell-on-Sea, the church of St Peter-on-the-Wall is a seventh-century place of worship, built using stones from the local Roman fort of Othona. At the foot of the peninsula is the little port of **Maldon** on the river Blackwater, with its triangular-towered church and Washington window: the town was home to the captain of the *Mayflower*. A tidal causeway leads out to **Northey Island** ⓘ *T01621-853142, www.nationaltrust.org.uk, open by appointment with the warden with 24 hrs' notice*. The island was the site of the Battle of Maldon in 991, celebrated in a remarkable Anglo-Saxon poem recounting the defeat of local hero Brythnoth and his men by the Vikings. Today it's a top birdwatching site.

Mersea Island

On the north side of the Blackwater estuary, about 10 miles east of Maldon, Mersea Island is reached over a low causeway liable to flooding at peak tides, and is also famous for its oysters. The Company Shed is a good place to eat them (see Restaurants below), looking south across the estuary to the sound of tinkling halyards in the boatyard.

Clacton and Frinton

East of Colchester, the main seaside resorts are Clacton-on-Sea and Frinton-on-Sea. Both are favourites with Londoners during the summer, comical in their appeal to different classes. Clacton's pier claims to be the largest in the country, and features a Seaquarium, rides and indoor bowling. Otherwise it's a very straightforward and well-maintained summer family holiday centre. Much more genteel, just up the coast, Frinton has an attractive grassy promenade, no amusement arcades and an orderly rank of neat little multicoloured beach huts stretching along the sandy beach.

Halfway to Colchester on the A133, in Elmstead Market, unpromising ground conditions were capitalized upon by top horticulturalist Beth Chatto over 40 years ago to create **Beth Chatto Gardens** ⓘ *Elmstead Market, T01206-822007, www.bethchatto.co.uk, Mon-Sat 0900-1600, Sun 1000-1600, open until 1700 in summer, £6.95, under-14s free*, with outstanding herbaceous borders, as well as dry Mediterranean and bog gardens. There's also a very highly rated nursery full of exotic plants if you want to try something similar at home.

Just to the north of Frinton, **Hamford Water** is a wide stretch of shallow water, mudflats and reedbeds covered by the tides. Popular with dinghy sailors, its maze of little creeks and islands was popularized by Arthur Ransome in *Swallows and Amazons*. Horsey Island sits in the middle, accessible at low tide only.

Stour Estuary

Further north, **Wrabness Nature Reserve** provides another wetland habitat worth exploring, near the old estuary villages of Mistley and Manningtree on the river Stour. Mistley Towers were designed by Robert Adam, now standing oddly on the ground bereft of their church in an enclosure beside the main road. At the mouth of the Stour, **Harwich** is an international ferry port with boats to Holland and Germany. A mile east of the main terminals, the old town is well worth a look around, sensitively restored since the war.

Essex listings

For hotel and restaurant price codes and other relevant information, see pages 9–12.

🛏 Where to stay

Saffron Walden, Thaxted, Great Dunmow and around *p84*

£££ The Starr, Market Pl, Great Dunmow, T01371-874321, www.the-starr.co.uk. Salubrious, expensive historic restaurant with rooms where Jamie Oliver cut his teeth. The 8 rooms are comfortably and traditionally furnished. Free Wi-Fi.

Colchester, Constable Country and around *p87*

££££ Maison Talbooth, Gun Hill, Dedham, T01206-323150, www.milsomhotels.com. Award-winning country house hotel with sumptuous rooms, a superb restaurant (see Restaurants below), outdoor heated pool and hot tub, and a tennis court. Free Wi-Fi.

£££ Mount Hall, London Rd, Great Horkesley, 4 miles north of Colchester, T01206-271359, www.mounthall.co.uk. Well situated for Constable country, this B&B is in a grand Queen Anne house set in beautiful landscaped grounds full of plants from the nearby Beth Chatto Gardens (see above) and a luxury yurt sleeping up to 4.

£££ North Hill Hotel, High St, Colchester, T01206-574001, www.northhillhotel.com. If an overnight stop in Colchester is necessary this place is your best bet, with friendly staff and comfortable rooms. Ask for a room at the back of the hotel as the front ones can be noisy. Discounted rates for the NCP car park opposite.

Essex Coast from Southend to Harwich *p89*

£££ The Pier at Harwich, The Quay, Harwich, T01206-322367, www.milsom hotels.com. Lovely waterfront historic Venetian-style hotel with great views of the harbour and well-appointed rooms. Free Wi-Fi.

££ Cap and Feathers, 8 South St, Tillingham, near Southminster, T01621-779212, http://capandfeathersfreehouse.co.uk. Attractive and cosy clapperboard pub with some excellent real ales.

🍴 Restaurants

Saffron Walden, Thaxted and around *p84*

££ The Cricketers, Clavering, 7 miles southwest of Saffron Walden, T01799-550442, www.thecricketers.co.uk. Award-winning charming pub run by the parents of Jamie Oliver, who started his career in their kitchens and whose organic gardens supply much of the pub's produce. Also has rooms (**£££**). Recommended.

££ Square 1, 15 High St, Great Dunmow, T01371-859922, www.square1 restaurant.co.uk. Unpretentious restaurant offering Mediterranean-influenced dishes with excellent value lunchtime and Monday evening set menus. The contemporary artwork on the walls is also for sale.

Colchester, Constable Country and around p87

£££ Le Talbooth, Gun Hill, Dedham, T01206-322367, www.milsomhotels.com. A short distance from **Maison Talbooth** hotel, see Where to stay above, which runs this restaurant. The haute cuisine option, with formal dining in a low, beamed room next to the river but within earshot of the A12.

££ The Angel Inn, Polstead St, Stoke-by-Nayland, T01206-263245, www.angelinnsuffolk.co.uk. This is a very popular pub in a 16th-century coaching inn on Nayland's main street, serving excellent food, including delicious cream teas. Friendly, efficient service. Also has attractive rooms (**£££**).

££ Baumann's Brasserie, Coggeshall, 4-6 Stoneham St, T01376-561453, www.baumanns brasserie.co.uk. Expensive and ambitious but distinctly a cut above most of the competition, run by Master Chef Mark Baumann.

££ The Sun Inn, High St, Dedham, T01206-323351, www.thesuninn dedham.com. Pub in a historic building with lots of exposed beams, log fires and wooden floorboards. The superb Italian-inspired dishes use seasonal ingredients and there are also beautifully decorated rooms (**£££**).

Essex Coast from Southend to Harwich p89

££ Pipe of Port, 84 High St, Southend, T01702-614606, www.pipeofport.co.uk. Bistro food served in an atmospheric candlelit cellar bar; probably the best on offer.

££-£ Company Shed, 129 Coast Rd, West Mersea, T01206-382700, www.the-company-shed.co.uk. Tue 0900-1700, Sun 1000-1700. No-frills popular eatery for the freshest seafood and shellfish. Bring your own bread and wine, last orders for eating taken at 1600. No advance booking so get there early. Recommended.

£ Blue Strawberry, Hatfield Peverel, T01245-381333, www.bluestrawberry bistro.co.uk. A sophisticated but good-value menu in a cosy French bistro setting.

🍸 Bars, pubs and clubs

Saffron Walden, Thaxted, Great Dunmow and around p84

The Compasses, Littley Green, Great Waltham, near Great Dunmow, T01245-362308, www.compasseslittley green.co.uk. Regularly voted CAMRA pub of the year, a Victorian drinking palace serving Essex real ales and huffers – huge well-filled buns. Now also offers rooms (**££**).

The Crown Inn, Little Walden, T01799-522475, www.thecrownlittle walden.co.uk. This welcoming pub has log fires in cold weather, good real ales (served from casks racked up behind the bar) and live jazz on a Wed evening. Good-value home made food (**£**) and rooms (**££**).

🚌 Transport

Colchester p87

Bus

Long distance **National Express** runs a direct service to **Ipswich** (40 mins). There are direct services to **London Victoria** (2 hrs 40 mins) and **Stansted airport** (50 mins), plus services to **Cambridge** (from 2 hrs 20 mins) via Stansted.

Rail

There is direct service to **Ipswich** (20 mins). There is also a direct service to **London Liverpool Street** (50 mins), which runs every 15 mins. There is no direct service to Cambridge or Stansted airport.

Happy Birthday

£1

Love
Annette.

WINDOWS OF TRUTH